KINGFISHER SCIENCE
ENCYCLOPEDIA
HUMAN
BIOLOGY

KINGFISHER

First published 2000 by Kingfisher

This updated editon published 2007 by Kingfisher
an imprint of Macmillan Children's Books
a division of Macmillan Publishers Limited
20 New Wharf Road, London N1 9RR
Basingstoke and Oxford
www.panmacmillan.com

Associated companies throughout the world

GENERAL EDITOR
Professor Charles Taylor, D. Sc., F.Inst.P.,
Emeritus Professor of Physics in the University of Wales

2005 EDITION CONSULTANT
Dr Mike Goldsmith

ISBN 978-0-7534-0436-2

3 5 7 9 8 6 4 2
2TS/1207/PROSP/UNIV(SCHOY)/128MA/C

A CIP catalogue record for this book is available from the British Library.

Printed in China

INTRODUCTION

In the 21st century, science and technology will increasingly dominate our lives. There will be many challenges, not only environmental, but ethical and moral as well. Science is the key subject for all children, and they need easy access to the scientific knowledge that will help them live in an increasingly demanding world.

Kingfisher Science Encyclopedia is divided into ten thematic volumes, each of them tackling a specific area of scientific interest and study. **Planet Earth** examines geological time, how oceans and mountains are formed, and Earth's atmosphere and weather systems. **Living Things** surveys life on our planet from the tiniest bacteria to the largest mammals, while **Human Biology** explores every part of the fantastic group of cells that is the human body. **Chemistry and the Elements** explains how solids, liquids and gases relate to each other, and interact, and **Materials and Technology** examines everyday materials and how they are used. **Light and Energy** looks at light, heat and colour; while human and machine power, sound and pressure are explored in the section called **Forces and Movement**. **Electricity and Electronics** delves into the increasingly technological world of power stations, telecommunications and information technology. In **Space and Time**, Earth is shown as a small part of an incredible Universe that we are only just beginning to explore, while **Conservation and the Environment** focuses on ways damage to the planet can be prevented.

The encyclopedia has been written by a team of specialist science authors and consultants led by Professor Charles Taylor, the first holder of the Royal Society's Michael Faraday Award for Contributions to the Understanding of Science in 1986, and this new edition has been fully updated by Dr Mike Goldsmith, head of Acoustics at the UK's National Physical Laboratory. Whether *Kingfisher Science Encyclopedia* is used for school work, or simply dipped into at random, it will add to knowledge, stimulate natural curiosity and creativity, and prepare the enquiring mind for an exciting future world.

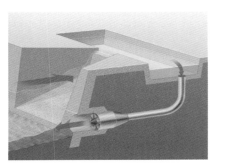

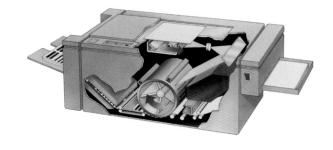

ACKNOWLEDGEMENTS

The publishers wish to thank the following for their contribution to the book:

Photographs (t = top; b = bottom; m = middle; l = left; r = right)
Page 2 tr V Rocher, Jerrican/Science Photo Library; 3 tr BSIP Meullemiestre/Science Photo Library; 4 bl Quest/Science Photo Library; 5 tr Richard Wehr/Custom Medical Stock Photo/Science Photo Library; 6 tl Jerry Young; bl Science Photo Library; 7 br CNRI/Science Photo Library; 8 tl Scott Camazine/Science Photo Library; 9 tm Philippe Plailly/Science Photo Library; tr Quest/Science Photo Library; 10 tl Laura Bosco/Sygma; 11 bl Don Fawcett/Science Photo Library; 13 ml CNRI/Science Photo Library; 14 tl Bridgeman Art Library; br Thomas Raupach/Still Pictures; 16 tr Larry Mulvehill/Science Photo Library; 17 tr Prof. P. Motta/G. Franchitto/University "La Sapienza", Rome/Science Photo Library; br Secchi-Lecague/Roussel-UCLAF/CNRI/Science Photo Library; 18 tl Kingfisher; tr CNRI/Science Photo Library; 21 tl BSIP GEMS EUROPE/Science Photo Library; tr Prof. P. Motta/Dept of Anatomy/University "La Sapienza", Rome/Science Photo Library; 23 t Rex Features; b Mark Clarke/Science Photo Library; 24 ml Quest/Science Photo Library; 25 bl CNRI/Science Photo Library; 26 tr National Cancer Institute/Science Photo Library; 28 bl Science Photo Library; 29 br CNRI/Science Photo Library; 30 tl Julian Holland; tr Julian Holland/Rainbows End Cafe, Glastonbury; b John Kelly/Tony Stone; 31 bl David Scharf/Science Photo Library; 32 bl Dr C. Liguory/CNRI/Science Photo Library; 33 tl David Scharf/Science Photo Library; br Eye of Science/Science Photo Library; 34 tl Kingfisher; 35 tl Simon Fraser, Royal Victoria Infirmary, Newcastle upon Tyne/Science Photo Library; 37 t Dept of Clinical Radiology, Salisbury District Hospital/Science Photo Library; 37 r V. Clement, Jerrican/Science Photo Library; 38 tr Kingfisher; 39 br Biophoto Associates/Science Photo Library; 40 tl Alain Dex, Publiphoto Diffusion/Science Photo Library; 41 b Juergen Berger, Max-Planck Institute/Science Photo Library; 42 tl James King-Holmes/Science Photo Library; tr CNRI/Science Photo Library; 43 tl John Walmsley; br John Walmsley; 44 tr Jorgen Schytte/Still Pictures; 45 tl CC Studio/Science Photo Library; br Matt Meadows, Peter Arnold Inc./Science Photo Library; 46 tr Deep Light Productions/Science Photo Library; ml Chris Bjornberg/Science Photo Library; br John Greim/Science Photo Library; 47 t Montreal Neuro. Institute/McGill University/CNRI/Science Photo Library; br Wellcome Dept. of Cognitive Neurology/Science Photo Library

Additional artwork: Jonathan Adams, Marianne Appleton, N. Ardley, Mike Atkinson, Graham Austen, Craig Austin, Richard Berridge, Louise Bolton, Simone Boni, Richard Bonson, Peter Bull, Julian Burgess, Robin Carter, Jim Channell, Kuo Kang Chen, Jeanne Colville, Tom Connell, Richard Coombes, Sandra Doyle, Richard Draper, David Eddington, Brin Edwards, David Etchell, Jeff Farrow, D. Fletcher, Eugene Fleury, Chris Forsey, Mark Franklin, Garden Studio, Sally Goodman, Jeremy Gower, Ray Grinaway, Terence Gubby, Terry Hadler, Alan Hancocks, A. Hardcastle, Hardlines, Ron Hayward, G. Hinks, Karen Hiscock, Christa Hooke, Lisa Horstman, Ian Howatson, Industrial Artists, Ian Jackson, Bridgette James, John James, E. Jenner, Ron Jobson, Kevin Jones, Felicity Kayes, Roger Kent, Elly and Christopher King, Terence Lambert, Adrian Lascom, Steve Latibeaudiere, Ruth Lindsay, Rachel Lockwood, Bernard Long, Mike Long, Chris Lyon, Kevin Madison, Mainline Design – Guy Smith, Alan Male, Maltings Partnership, Janos Marffy, Shane Marsh, Josephine Martin, Eve Melavish, Simon Mendez, Carol Merryman, Ian Moores, Patrick Murey, William Oliver, R. Payne, Bruce Pearson, David Phipps, Jonathan Potter, Malcolm Porter, Sebastian Quigley, E. Rice, Paul Richardson, John Ridyard, Steve Roberts, B. Robinson, Eric Robson, Mike Rolfe, David Russell, Valerie Sangster, Mike Saunders, Nick Shewning, Chris Shields, Mike Stacey, Roger Stewart, Lucy Su, Mike Taylor, Simon Teg, George Thompson, Ian Thompson, Linda Thursby, Guy Troughton, Simon Turvey, T.K.Uayte, Ross Watton, Phil Wear, Paul Weare, David Webb, Steve Weston, Graham White, Peter Wilkinson, Ann Winterbotham, John Woodcock, David Wright.

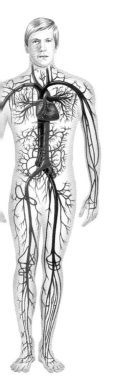

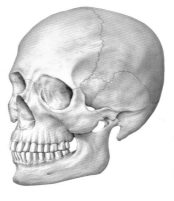

CONTENTS

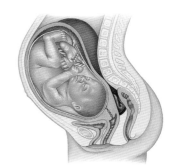

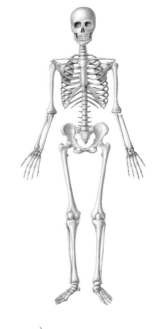

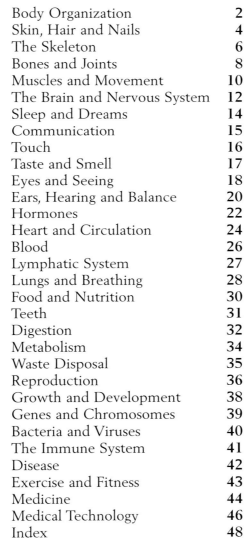

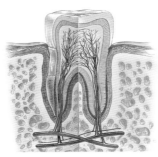

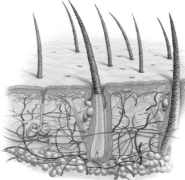

BODY ORGANIZATION

The human body consists of more than 50 trillion microscopic living units, called cells. These cells perform specific tasks to ensure that the body works.

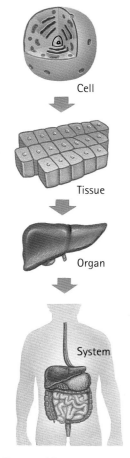

Cell

Tissue

Organ

System

Groups of liver cells form a tissue. This tissue with others make up the organ called the liver. Together, the liver and other linked organs make up the digestive system.

The human body is organized according to a hierarchy, or sequence, of different levels of complexity, starting from simple molecules right up to the body itself. Molecules such as carbohydrates, lipids, nucleic acids and proteins form the building blocks from which cells are made. They also take part in the chemical reactions collectively called metabolism. The body's metabolism interacts with the body's building blocks to form tiny living units called cells. To stay alive and give the body energy, each cell needs a constant supply of food and oxygen.

Individual cells that are similar in structure and function join together to form tissues. These perform different roles in the body. Several different types of tissues form structures called organs, each of which have a specific task or tasks. Organs include the eyes, kidneys, liver, lungs and stomach. For example, the role of the stomach is to store and break down food during digestion. The stomach works with other linked organs to form the digestive system. This not only digests food, but also absorbs useful nutrients from food into the bloodstream and eliminates any waste. The digestive system is one of twelve systems, all of which work together to ensure that the body carries out the functions it needs to survive.

Each young person in this photograph looks completely different. Apart from the differences between males and females, however, they all share the same basic body structure, which works in exactly the same way.

TISSUES

The body is made up of four basic types of tissues. Epithelial tissues are tightly packed cells that form leakproof linings to surfaces such as the skin and the lining of the digestive system. Connective tissues hold the body together and provide a framework. They include cartilage and bone. Muscular tissues consist of cells that contract (tighten) to move the body. Nervous tissue, in the brain and nerves, consists of a network of cells that carry electrical signals. Most organs contain all four types of tissue. Within tissues, cells are surrounded by tissue fluid. The fluid provides cells with a stable environment, delivers oxygen and food to the cells and removes waste products.

BODY SYSTEMS

There are 12 major systems in the human body. Seven of these are shown here. The systems not shown here include the respiratory system, integumentary system (skin, hair and nails), male and female reproductive systems, urinary system and the immune system. Each system carries out one or more processes essential for life. For example, the circulatory system – the heart, blood vessels and blood – delivers food and oxygen to all body cells and removes their waste products.

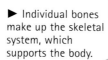

► Individual bones make up the skeletal system, which supports the body.

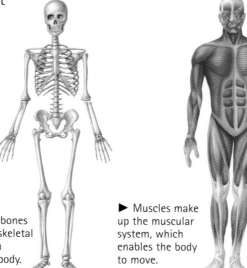

► Muscles make up the muscular system, which enables the body to move.

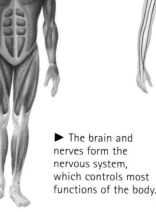

► The brain and nerves form the nervous system, which controls most functions of the body.

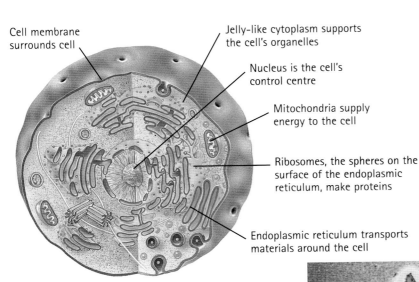

Cell membrane surrounds cell

Jelly-like cytoplasm supports the cell's organelles

Nucleus is the cell's control centre

Mitochondria supply energy to the cell

Ribosomes, the spheres on the surface of the endoplasmic reticulum, make proteins

Endoplasmic reticulum transports materials around the cell

Although different cells come in various shapes and sizes, they look very similar inside. Organelles ('tiny organs') inside the cell have specific functions. They all work together to produce a living cell.

During a type of cell division known as mitosis, the nucleus (dark area in the diagram) of the parent cell (1) divides first (2), then the cytoplasm divides (3) and two identical daughter cells are produced (4).

CELLS

Although different cells perform different tasks, they all share the same structure. A plasma membrane separates each cell from its surroundings and allows material into and out of the cell. Inside the cell, tiny organelles – the microscopic equivalent of the body's organs – float in a watery jelly called cytoplasm. Organelles do different things, but they all cooperate to produce a living cell. The most important organelle is the nucleus, the cell's control centre. The nucleus contains genetic material in the form of deoxyribonucleic acid (DNA). This provides the blueprint for building and running the cell. Other organelles include mitochondria, ribosomes and endoplasmic reticulum.

Cells reproduce by dividing in one of two ways. Mitosis, which occurs throughout the body, enables the body to grow and repair itself by replacing worn-out cells. Meiosis, which occurs only in the testes and ovaries, produces sex cells – sperm and eggs – that take part in reproduction.

▲ This magnified image shows a cell called a lymphocyte. These cells are found in blood. The nucleus of a lymphocyte takes up much of the space inside the cell. Lymphocytes play a vital part in defending the body against disease.

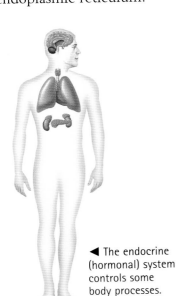

◄ The endocrine (hormonal) system controls some body processes.

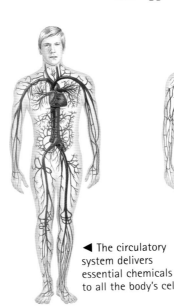

◄ The circulatory system delivers essential chemicals to all the body's cells.

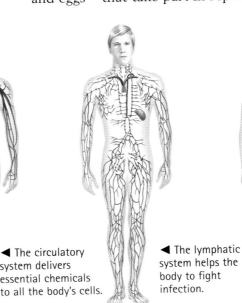

◄ The lymphatic system helps the body to fight infection.

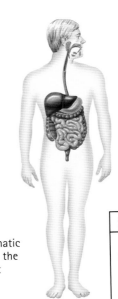

◄ The digestive system digests foods and absorbs nutrients into the body.

SEE ALSO

12–13 The brain and nervous system, 24–25 Heart and circulation, 27 Lymphatic system, 41 The immune system

SKIN, HAIR AND NAILS

A person's skin, hair and nails are the visible parts of the body. They form a protective barrier between the inside of the body and its surroundings.

Whether hair is curly, wavy or straight depends on the shape of the hair follicle. Curly hairs have a flat shaft and grow from slotlike hair follicles.

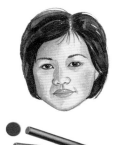

If straight hair is viewed through a microscope, it is seen to have a round shaft. Straight hair grows from hair follicles that have a round opening.

Wavy hair is oval in cross-section, as seen when a hair is cut across its shaft. Wavy hair grows from hair follicles that have an oval opening.

The skin is a living, protective overcoat that weighs up to 4 kilograms and can repair itself if cut or torn. The thinnest skin, on the eyelids, is about 1 millimetre thick. The thickest, on the soles of the feet, is about 4 millimetres thick.

Skin has two layers: the epidermis and dermis. The epidermis covers the skin's surface. Its upper layers consist of scalelike, dead cells filled with a waterproof protein called keratin. These dead cells are continually worn away and replaced by cells that form in the lower epidermis. Cells here also produce melanin, the brown pigment that colours the skin. Ridges on the skin of the fingers aid gripping and can mark surfaces with patterns called fingerprints.

The thicker dermis contains blood vessels, sweat glands, hair follicles and sensors that detect pressure, pain, temperature and touch. It also contains sebaceous glands, which secrete oily sebum onto skin and hairs to soften and waterproof them.

Skin has many functions. Skin is waterproof. It helps the body to maintain a steady temperature of 37°C. It provides a germproof barrier to protect the body from disease. Melanin prevents harmful rays in sunlight from reaching the dermis.

The surface of healthy skin, as seen under the microscope, is covered by tiny skin flakes. These are constantly shed from the surface of the epidermis as it is worn away and replaced. A person loses about 4 kg of skin flakes each year, which form part of household dust.

Fingerprints are unique to an individual, and if left at the scene of a crime, help to identify criminals. Permanent records of criminals' fingerprints are kept by the police.

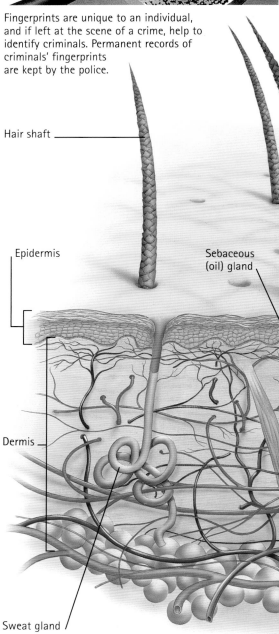

Hair shaft

Epidermis

Sebaceous (oil) gland

Dermis

Sweat gland

HAIR FACTS

Millions of hairs cover the body, including more than 100,000 on the top of the head. Scalp hairs cut heat loss from the head and protect it from harmful rays in sunlight. The lips, the palms of the hands and the soles of the feet have no hair.

There are two types of hair. Fine vellus hair covers the bodies of men, women and children, while coarser hairs grow on the scalp and in men's facial hair. Hairs grow from pits in the dermis called follicles. Cells at the base of the follicle divide and push the hair shaft upwards. The cells in the hair shaft are dead and filled with the tough protein called keratin. Scalp hairs grow about 1 centimetre each month. The colour of hair depends on how much of the pigment melanin is present.

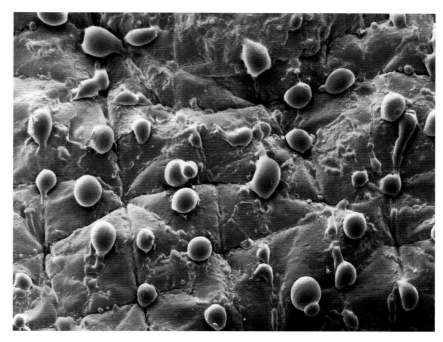

◄ Although most skin is only 2 mm thick, it has a complex structure. The epidermis forms a thin, protective surface that is continually worn away and replaced. Beneath it, the thicker dermis contains hair follicles, from which hairs grow; blood vessels, which supply skin cells with food and oxygen; nerve endings, which detect pain, pressure, temperature and touch; and sweat glands, which release cooling sweat.

Sweat pore (opening)

Scales on hair shaft

Tough outer layer of epidermis

Nerve ending

Nerve fibre

Muscle that makes hair erect

Hair follicle

Blood vessels

Layer of fat

Hair root

▲ Droplets of sweat, magnified 26 times, emerge from the openings, or pores, of sweat glands onto the surface of the skin. Sweat is released when the body is hot. It evaporates from the surface and cools down the body.

NAIL FACTS

Nails cover and protect the sensitive tips of the fingers and toes. They are useful to scratch itches and to help pick up small objects. It does not hurt when nails are cut because they are made of dead cells filled with the protein keratin.

Each nail consists of a free edge, the part that is cut; a nail body, the main part that looks pink; and the nail root, which is embedded in the skin beneath the cuticle. In the nail root, living cells divide and push forward, making the nail grow. Nails grow about 5 millimetres each month, slower in winter than in summer, and faster in the dominant hand – the right hand in right-handed people.

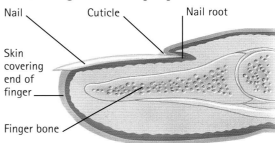

Nail   Cuticle   Nail root

Skin covering end of finger

Finger bone

The nail grows from three places – the root at the base of the fingertip, the skin beneath the nail and the bone inside the finger.

SEE ALSO

16 Touch, 26 Blood, 40 Bacteria and viruses, 42 Disease

THE SKELETON

The skeleton is a flexible framework that shapes and supports the body, protects vital organs such as the brain and anchors the muscles that move the body.

For centuries, bones were regarded as lifeless structures whose main aim was to support the active softer tissues around them. Gradually, scientists realized that bones are very much alive. Indeed, they have their own blood vessels and are constantly being rebuilt and reshaped.

The skeleton is not just a supportive framework for the body. Flexible joints between different bones enable the bones to move when pulled by muscles. The skeleton also protects vital organs such as the brain inside the skull. Bones themselves act as a store of calcium. This mineral is essential for muscles and nerves to work properly. Bones also make different types of blood cells. The skeleton contains cartilage, which covers the ends of bones in joints, and forms part of the skeletal system itself in the ear and nose, and between the sternum (breastbone) and ribs.

There are more than 20 bones in the human skull. Together, they provide a number of clues about the shape of the face and head. Scientists can use these clues to rebuild muscles and skin around the skull using clay. As a result, experts can recreate the faces of people who died long ago.

TYPES OF BONE

The four main kinds of bone are classified according to their shape and size. Long bones, such as the femur (thighbone), are adapted to withstand stress. Short bones include the wrist bones. Flat bones, such as the ribs, are often protective bones. Irregular bones include the vertebrae.

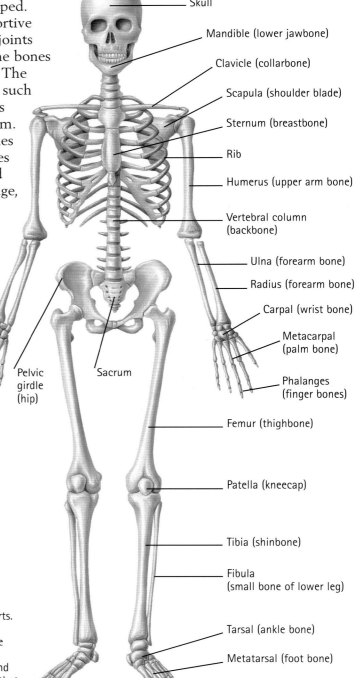

- Skull
- Mandible (lower jawbone)
- Clavicle (collarbone)
- Scapula (shoulder blade)
- Sternum (breastbone)
- Rib
- Humerus (upper arm bone)
- Vertebral column (backbone)
- Ulna (forearm bone)
- Radius (forearm bone)
- Carpal (wrist bone)
- Metacarpal (palm bone)
- Phalanges (finger bones)
- Femur (thighbone)
- Patella (kneecap)
- Tibia (shinbone)
- Fibula (small bone of lower leg)
- Tarsal (ankle bone)
- Metatarsal (foot bone)
- Phalanges (toe bones)
- Pelvic girdle (hip)
- Sacrum

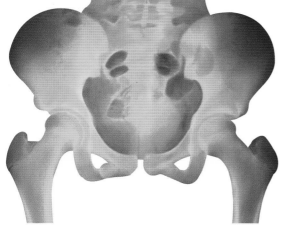

▲ This X-ray shows the pelvis (hips) of a 13-year-old girl. The image includes the hip bones, femurs (thighbones) and the lower part of the vertebral column. X-rays are commonly used to provide images of parts of the skeleton.

▶ An adult skeleton is made up of 206 bones. It can be divided into two parts. The axial skeleton forms the main axis of the body and consists of 80 bones that make up the skull, vertebral column (backbone) and ribs. This part of the skeleton protects the brain, spinal cord, heart and lungs. The appendicular skeleton consists of the upper and lower limbs and the pectoral (shoulder) and pelvic (hip) girdles that attach them to the axial skeleton. Of the 126 bones that make up the appendicular skeleton, all but 20 are found in the hands and feet.

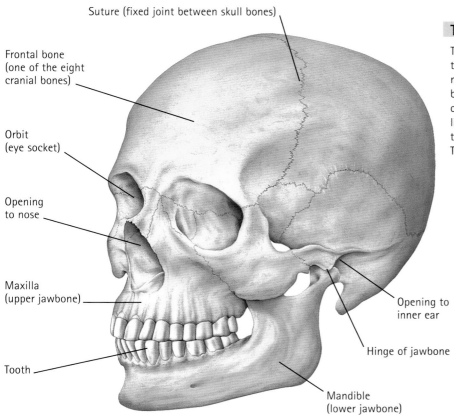

Suture (fixed joint between skull bones)

Frontal bone
(one of the eight
cranial bones)

Orbit
(eye socket)

Opening
to nose

Maxilla
(upper jawbone)

Tooth

Opening to
inner ear

Hinge of jawbone

Mandible
(lower jawbone)

THE HUMAN SKULL

The skull forms the basic shape of the head and protects
the brain. It consists of 22 bones. Eight cranial bones
make up the cranium, which supports and protects the
brain. There are 14 facial bones that form the structure
of the face. All but the mandible (lower jawbone) are
linked by fixed joints called sutures. The mandible is able
to move freely, allowing the mouth to open and close.
The skull also houses three pairs of ossicles or ear bones.

'Exploded' view of skull

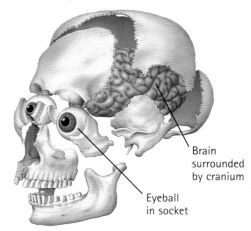

Brain
surrounded
by cranium

Eyeball
in socket

AXIAL SKELETON

The axial skeleton consists of the skull,
vertebral column (backbone), ribs and
sternum. The skull houses the brain and
the major sense organs – the eyes, ears,
tongue and nose. It also contains openings
to the digestive and respiratory systems.
The flexible, S-shaped spinal column is
made up of 26 irregular bones called
vertebrae, which support the entire body.
Muscles and ligaments attached to bony
projections on the vertebrae help to keep
the backbone upright. Seven cervical
vertebrae support the neck and head,
twelve thoracic vertebrae form joints with
the ribs and five lumbar vertebrae carry
most of the body's weight. The sacrum
and coccyx are fused vertebrae that
connect the spine to the pelvic girdle.

The ribcage protects the thoracic
(chest) organs and also aids breathing. It is
formed by the sternum (breastbone) and
twelve pairs of curved, flattened ribs. The
ribs form a joint with the thoracic vertebrae
at one end. The upper seven, or true, ribs
are connected to the sternum by flexible
costal (rib) cartilages. The next three,
called false ribs, are connected to the true
ribs. The lowest two ribs (floating ribs) are
attached only to the thoracic vertebrae.

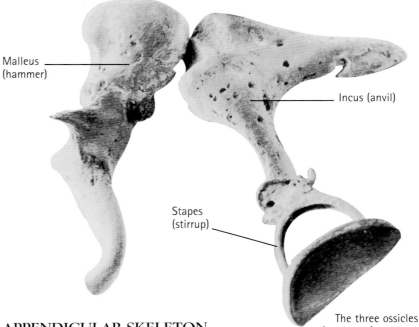

Malleus
(hammer)

Incus (anvil)

Stapes
(stirrup)

APPENDICULAR SKELETON

The appendicular skeleton is made up of
the bones in the arms and legs and also
girdles that link them to the body. The
pectoral (shoulder) girdle consists of the
scapula and clavicle. The pelvic (hip)
girdle carries the weight of the upper
body. The hands and feet contain many
small bones. The hands can manipulate
objects. The feet help to balance the body.

The three ossicles
(ear bones) are the
smallest bones in the
body. The ossicles are
located within the
temporal bone on each
side of the skull.

SEE ALSO

8–9 Bones and joints,
10–11 Muscles and
movement, 20–1 Ears,
hearing and balance

BONES AND JOINTS

Bone is living tissue that is both strong and light. The 206 bones that make up the skeletal system are linked together at joints, most of which move freely.

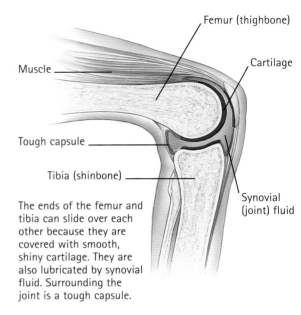

Femur (thighbone)

Cartilage

Muscle

Tough capsule

Tibia (shinbone)

Synovial (joint) fluid

The ends of the femur and tibia can slide over each other because they are covered with smooth, shiny cartilage. They are also lubricated by synovial fluid. Surrounding the joint is a tough capsule.

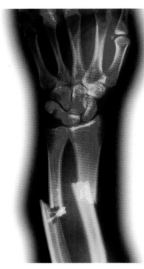

This X-ray clearly shows a fracture of the ulna (at left) and radius (at right). The fractured ends of the bones need to be put back in place by a doctor so that they join properly as the bones heal. The hand bones are shown at the top of the picture.

There are few structures that can rival bone in terms of its strength and lightness. All bones are made up of a hard material, called matrix, that contains widely spaced bone cells called osteocytes. Bone matrix consists of two main parts – a protein called collagen provides flexibility, and mineral salts, in particular calcium phosphate, provide strength. Together, these two components make bone as strong as steel but five times as light.

Matrix has two forms in bones: hard, compact bone forms the outer layer; lighter, spongy bone forms the inner layer. Long bones, such as the femur, contain a central cavity filled with bone marrow. This jelly-like material also fills the spaces within spongy bone. Red bone marrow, found in the skull, ribs and pelvis, is responsible for making red and white blood cells. Yellow bone marrow, found in the long bones of adults, stores fat.

BREAK AND REPAIR

Bones fracture if they are put under stress. If this occurs, a blood clot forms between the broken ends, and bone cells secrete a new matrix. Fractures are compound (open) if the bones project through the skin or simple (closed) if they do not.

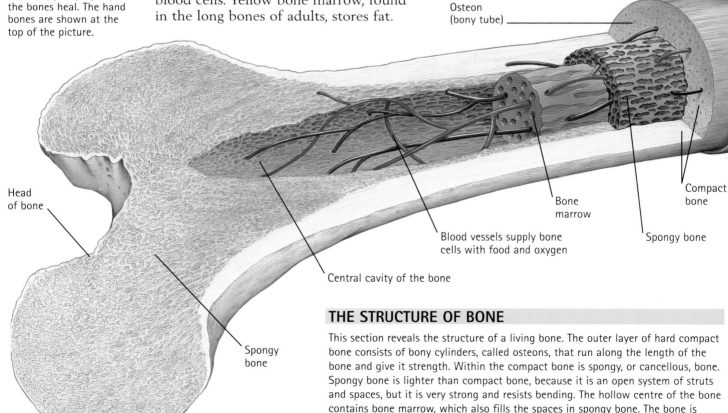

Head of bone

Spongy bone

Central cavity of the bone

Blood vessels supply bone cells with food and oxygen

Osteon (bony tube)

Bone marrow

Spongy bone

Compact bone

THE STRUCTURE OF BONE

This section reveals the structure of a living bone. The outer layer of hard compact bone consists of bony cylinders, called osteons, that run along the length of the bone and give it strength. Within the compact bone is spongy, or cancellous, bone. Spongy bone is lighter than compact bone, because it is an open system of struts and spaces, but it is very strong and resists bending. The hollow centre of the bone contains bone marrow, which also fills the spaces in spongy bone. The bone is protected by a tough membrane called the periosteum. Blood vessels pass through the periosteum and supply osteocytes (bone cells) with food and oxygen.

JOINTS

Joints, or articulations, are the points at which two bones meet. They are classified into three main groups – fixed, slightly movable and synovial – according to the amount of movement each permits. Fixed joints, as their name suggests, allow no movement. The sutures between the bones of the skull are examples of fixed joints. Their jagged edges are similar to the pieces of a jigsaw, locking the skull bones firmly together. Each tooth is another example of a fixed joint. Teeth are firmly locked in their sockets so that they do not move when food is chewed. Slightly movable joints allow limited movement between adjacent bones. These joints are found between vertebrae. Adjacent vertebra are separated by an intervertebral disc made of fibrocartilage. This allows partial movement between vertebrae. Collectively these joints give the backbone flexibility and allow it to bend backwards and forwards and from side to side.

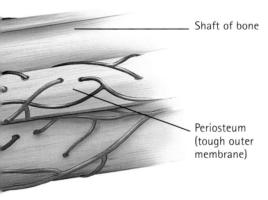

Shaft of bone

Periosteum (tough outer membrane)

SYNOVIAL JOINTS

Most joints – including the knee, elbow, knuckles, hip and shoulder – are freely movable, or synovial, joints. Synovial joints permit a wide range of movements. All synovial joints share the same basic structure. Bone ends are covered with glassy cartilage. Where the bones meet, they are separated by a synovial cavity filled with synovial fluid. Together, the cartilage and synovial fluid 'oil' the joint and reduce friction, producing a smooth movement. A joint capsule surrounds each synovial joint. Its inner membrane secretes synovial fluid. The outer part is continuous with tough straps, called ligaments, that hold the joint together.

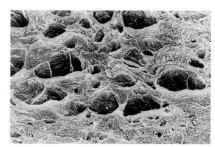

A magnified cross-section of compact bone from the femur reveals two osteons. In the middle of each osteon is a central channel that carries blood vessels. Dark spaces in the osteon contain bone cells.

This magnified image of spongy bone from a bone in the foot looks very different to compact bone (at left). It consists of hard struts separated by linked spaces filled with bone marrow.

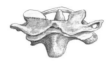

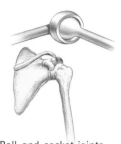

In a pivot joint, the end of one bone rotates within a space formed by another bone. At the top of the backbone, the atlas (first vertebra) rotates around the axis (second vertebra). This allows the head to turn from side to side.

A hinge joint works like a door hinge. The cylindrical end of one bone fits into the curved end of another bone. Hinge joints allow movement up and down but not from side to side. The knee (above) is an example of a hinge joint.

Ball-and-socket joints, such as in the shoulder (above), are the body's most flexible joints. The ball-shaped end of one bone fits into the cup-shaped socket of another bone, allowing movement in all directions.

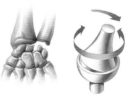

In the saddle joint at the base of the thumb, the U-shaped ends of wrist and thumb bones fit together, permitting movement backwards and forwards and from side to side. This joint also allows the thumb to touch the tip of each finger.

Ellipsoidal, or condyloid, joints are found in the knuckles and between the lower arm and wrist bones. The egg-shaped end of one bone fits into the oval cup of another bone, allowing movement backwards and forwards and from side to side.

In a gliding, or plane, joint, the surfaces of each bone are level, allowing the bones to make short movements by sliding over each other. Gliding joints are found between carpals (wrist bones) in each hand and tarsals (heel bones) in each foot.

RANGE OF MOVEMENT

The shape of bone ends, the arrangement of muscles and the tightness of ligaments holding the joint together all determine the range of movement at a joint. The straightening and bending of the arm at the elbow is an example of extension (straightening) and flexion (bending). The raising and lowering of the lower jaw when chewing food is an example of elevation (lifting) and depression (lowering).

SEE ALSO

6–7 The skeleton, 10–11 Muscles and movement, 38 Growth and development

MUSCLES AND MOVEMENT

Every movement, from blinking an eye to running in a race, is produced by the body's muscles. Muscles are made of cells that have the unique ability to contract.

All the actions involved in skipping, such as moving the arms and hands, bending the knees and lifting the feet, are produced by skeletal muscles. Instructed by the brain, these muscles pull the skeleton to produce coordinated movements.

Three types of muscle are found in the body: skeletal, smooth and cardiac. Sprinting uses skeletal muscle, digestion requires smooth muscle, and a heartbeat involves cardiac muscle. As their name suggests, skeletal muscles move the bones of the skeleton and help support the body. The body has over 640 skeletal muscles that cover the skeleton and give the body overall shape. Skeletal muscles make up 40 per cent of the body's weight. They range in size from the powerful quadriceps femoris (thigh muscle) to the tiny stapedius in the ear. Tough cords called tendons attach the end of the skeletal muscle to the bone. Muscles extend across joints. When the muscles contract, bones move relative to one another.

HOW MUSCLES WORK

Skeletal muscle cells, or fibres, are long, thin and packed with lots of parallel strands called myofibrils. Myofibrils contain two protein filaments – actin and myosin – which make skeletal muscle fibres look stripy. When a muscle receives a message from the brain along a nerve, the filaments slide past each other, making the fibre shorter, and the muscle contracts. Muscles can only pull, not push; they usually work in pairs, each pulling bones in the opposite direction.

Most muscles work in pairs, each with an action that is antagonistic to (opposes) the other. In the upper arm, for example, biceps brachii contracts (with triceps brachii relaxed) to bend the arm, while triceps brachii contracts (with biceps brachii relaxed) to straighten it.

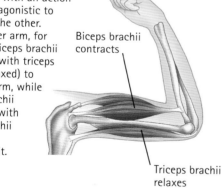

Biceps brachii contracts

Triceps brachii relaxes

Biceps brachii relaxes

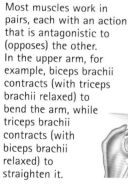

Triceps brachii contracts

▶ The body's skeletal muscles are arranged in overlapping layers. The muscles that are just below the skin are called superficial. Beneath these are the deep muscles. This anterior (front) view of the body shows some important superficial muscles and their actions. Muscles are given Latin names for different reasons. These include their action (flexor or extensor), their shape (deltoid means triangular), their relative size (maximus means largest) or their location (frontalis covers the frontal bone).

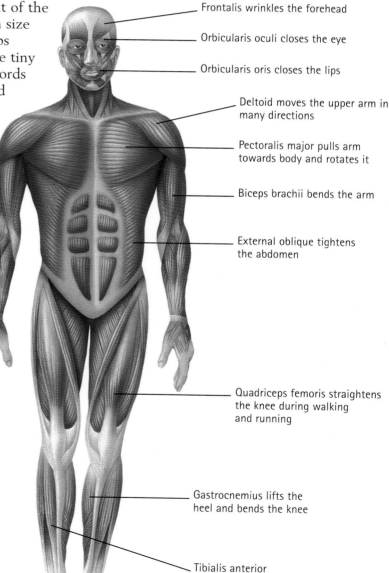

Frontalis wrinkles the forehead

Orbicularis oculi closes the eye

Orbicularis oris closes the lips

Deltoid moves the upper arm in many directions

Pectoralis major pulls arm towards body and rotates it

Biceps brachii bends the arm

External oblique tightens the abdomen

Quadriceps femoris straightens the knee during walking and running

Gastrocnemius lifts the heel and bends the knee

Tibialis anterior straightens or lifts foot

Muscle straightens wrist

Tendon from muscle straightens thumb

The muscles that flex and extend the wrist and fingers are located in the forearm. These muscles are attached to bones in the hands and fingers by long tendons. These tendons can be seen and felt on the back of the hand. A fibrous band, called the retinaculum, encircles the wrist and keeps the tendons in place. Muscles in the hand itself move the thumb and the fingers.

Thumb of right hand

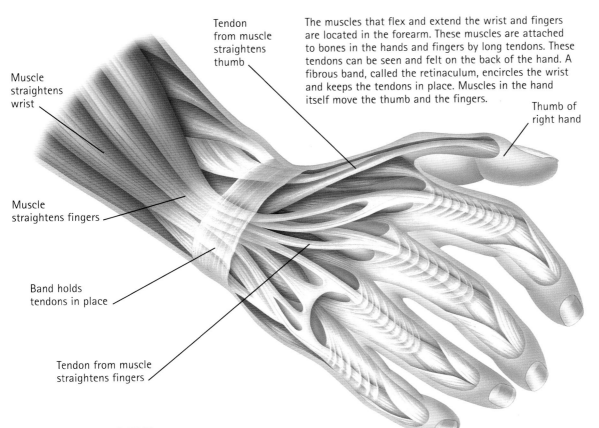

Muscle straightens fingers

Band holds tendons in place

Tendon from muscle straightens fingers

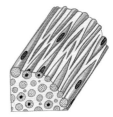

Skeletal muscle fibres

Smooth muscle fibres

Cardiac muscle fibres

SMOOTH MUSCLE

Smooth, or involuntary, muscle is found mainly in the walls of hollow organs such as the oesophagus and bladder. Smooth muscle is vital to involuntary processes such as moving food along the alimentary canal during digestion (peristalsis). The short, tapering fibres of smooth muscle are packed into sheets and contract smoothly and rhythmically under the control of the autonomic nervous system – a person cannot consciously cause them to contract.

CARDIAC MUSCLE

Cardiac muscle is found only in the heart and makes up a large part of its structure. Its branched, striped fibres form an interconnected network. These fibres contract spontaneously without the need for an outside stimulus from the nervous system. Cardiac muscle contracts nonstop over 2.5 billion times in an average lifetime to pump blood around the body.

Muscle fibres differ in their appearance. Skeletal muscle fibres are long and striped. Smooth muscle fibres are short and tapered. Cardiac muscle fibres are striped and branched.

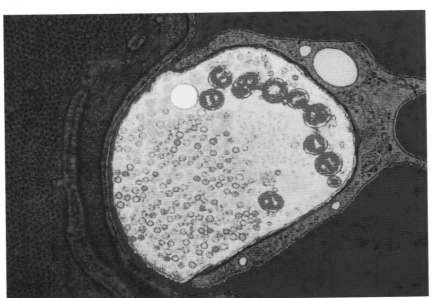

Sheath

Sheath

Muscle fibre (cell)

◄ A neuromuscular junction (here magnified 30,800 times) is where the end of a nerve fibre (yellow) meets a muscle fibre (red). When a nerve impulse arrives at a nerve ending, chemicals are released to make the muscle contract.

Skeletal muscle fibres are arranged in bundles that run along a muscle. Myofibrils inside each fibre consist of filaments that interact to make the muscle contract.

SEE ALSO

6–7 The skeleton,
12–13 The brain and nervous system

THE BRAIN AND NERVOUS SYSTEM

Billions of nerve cells, called neurons, link up to form the body's communication network, called the nervous system. The nervous system is controlled by the brain.

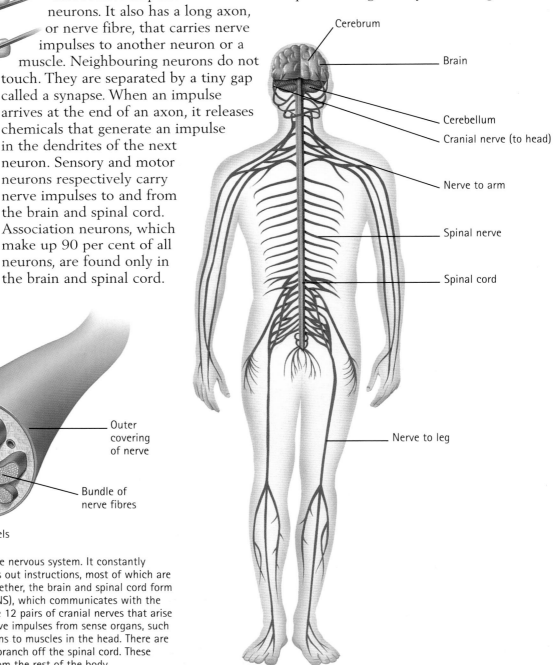

Spinal cord

Spinal nerve

Vertebra (bony segment of backbone)

The spinal cord extends from the base of the brain to the lower back. It is protected by the vertebrae. Spinal nerves branch off the spinal cord and carry nerve impulses to and from parts of the body.

Nerves consist of bundles of sensory neurons – which carry nerve impulses from sensors to the brain and spinal cord – and motor neurons – which carry nerve impulses from the brain and spinal cord to the muscles.

The neuron is the basic unit of the nervous system. It is long, thin and transmits electrical signals, called nerve impulses, along its length. The cell body of the neuron is much like any other cell. It has many branched endings called dendrites that receive impulses from other neurons. It also has a long axon, or nerve fibre, that carries nerve impulses to another neuron or a muscle. Neighbouring neurons do not touch. They are separated by a tiny gap called a synapse. When an impulse arrives at the end of an axon, it releases chemicals that generate an impulse in the dendrites of the next neuron. Sensory and motor neurons respectively carry nerve impulses to and from the brain and spinal cord. Association neurons, which make up 90 per cent of all neurons, are found only in the brain and spinal cord.

Nerve fibre

Outer covering of nerve

Bundle of nerve fibres

Blood vessels

► The brain controls the entire nervous system. It constantly receives information and sends out instructions, most of which are relayed by the spinal cord. Together, the brain and spinal cord form the central nervous system (CNS), which communicates with the body through nerves. There are 12 pairs of cranial nerves that arise from the brain. Most relay nerve impulses from sense organs, such as the eyes, or carry instructions to muscles in the head. There are 31 pairs of spinal nerves that branch off the spinal cord. These relay nerve impulses to and from the rest of the body.

SPINAL CORD

Essentially, the spinal cord is an extension of the brain. It is about 45 centimetres long and extends from the brain to the lower back. Spinal nerves along its length relay information between the brain and body. It also plays a vital role in reflexes. If a person touches a sharp object, for example, nerve impulses pass from the fingertip, through the spinal cord, directly to the upper arm muscles and instantly pull the finger away from danger.

Cerebrum

Brain

Cerebellum

Cranial nerve (to head)

Nerve to arm

Spinal nerve

Spinal cord

Nerve to leg

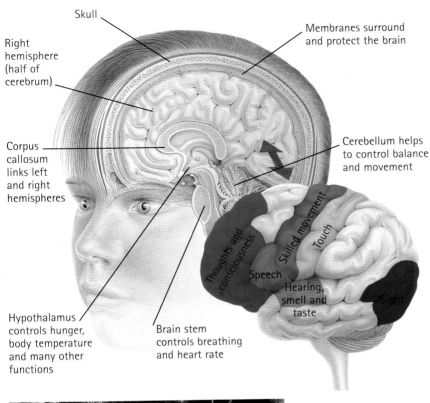

- Skull
- Right hemisphere (half of cerebrum)
- Corpus callosum links left and right hemispheres
- Hypothalamus controls hunger, body temperature and many other functions
- Membranes surround and protect the brain
- Cerebellum helps to control balance and movement
- Brain stem controls breathing and heart rate

Thoughts and consciousness
Speech
Skilled movement
Touch
Hearing, smell and taste
Sight

INSIDE THE BRAIN

The brain is made up of three main regions. The brain stem automatically controls essential functions such as breathing and heartbeat. The cerebellum coordinates balance, posture and movement. The cerebrum is divided into two halves called hemispheres, linked by the corpus callosum. Different parts of each hemisphere have different functions. Sensory areas process nerve impulses from sense organs such as the eyes. Motor areas relay instructions to muscles, producing movement and speech. Association areas, such as the front of the cerebrum, make people conscious and able to think. Beneath the cerebrum, the hypothalamus regulates conditions inside the body through the autonomic nervous system.

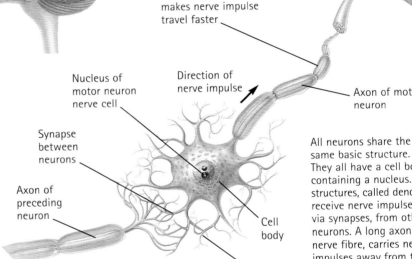

- Muscle
- Nerve-muscle junction
- Insulating sheath makes nerve impulse travel faster
- Nucleus of motor neuron nerve cell
- Direction of nerve impulse
- Axon of motor neuron
- Synapse between neurons
- Axon of preceding neuron
- Cell body
- Dendrite

All neurons share the same basic structure. They all have a cell body containing a nucleus. Thin structures, called dendrites, receive nerve impulses, via synapses, from other neurons. A long axon, or nerve fibre, carries nerve impulses away from the cell body. The cell body of this motor neuron is located in the central nervous system (CNS). It transmits nerve impulses to parts of the body instructing them to do something. For example, a nerve impulse to a muscle may cause it to contract. Similarly, a nerve impulse to a gland may cause it to release a secretion.

This image, which is magnified 494 times, shows association neurons from the cerebral cortex, the thin, outer part of the cerebrum (the 'thinking' part of the brain). Each neuron is linked to thousands of others.

BRAIN

The brain is made up of over 100 billion neurons. Each one communicates with thousands of other neurons to produce a complex communication and control network. The brain receives information about conditions both inside and outside the body, processes and stores this information and issues instructions based on what it has learned. The hypothalamus and brain stem control automatic processes such as breathing. The cerebellum regulates smooth body movements. The cerebral hemispheres control thought, imagination, memory, speech, emotion, sight, hearing, smell, taste and touch.

PARTS OF THE NERVOUS SYSTEM

The nervous system has two main parts: the brain and spinal cord form the central nervous system (CNS) and the nerves form the peripheral nervous system (PNS). Within the PNS, sensory neurons transmit nerve impulses from sense organs to the brain. Motor neurons transmit instructions from the brain and are of two types. Those of the somatic nervous system are under voluntary control and stimulate skeletal muscles to contract. Those of the autonomic nervous system (ANS) regulate processes inside the body such as breathing and digestion. The ANS has two divisions: sympathetic and parasympathetic. These have opposite effects and keep the body in a stable state.

SEE ALSO
10–11 Muscles and movement, 14 Sleep and dreams, 46–7 Medical technology

SLEEP AND DREAMS

Sleep takes up about one third of a person's life. It allows the body to rest and the brain to process information taken in during the previous day.

This picture, called *Lena's Dream*, is an artist's attempt to convey the strange mixture of images that people see in their dreams. Here a child is asleep in bed but in the middle of a field. Dreams occur while the brain is sorting out all the experiences of the previous day. In the altered consciousness of sleep, these memories are distorted into dreams.

Sleep occurs naturally as part of a 24-hour cycle of wakefulness and sleep. It is a state of altered consciousness from which a person can be easily aroused. Sleep is important – people deprived of sleep become tired, confused and experience hallucinations.

Evidence for events that occur during sleep comes from scientists who observe the behaviour of sleeping subjects and use an electroencephalograph (EEG) to measure their brainwaves.

Whether we are awake or sleeping, brainwaves are produced constantly by the electrical 'traffic' that passes between the billions of neurons in the brain. Different brainwaves occur according to whether someone is awake, mentally alert, falling asleep or in deep sleep. Dreams are the events that someone experiences during sleep. They are probably a side effect of the brain putting in order the experiences of the previous day, and storing them in the memory.

DEEP SLEEP AND DREAMING SLEEP

Sleep follows a pattern of events that occur in a certain order and repeat themselves. When people fall asleep, they experience four stages of sleep from nearly awake to deep, or NREM (nonrapid-eye-movement), sleep. The heart and breathing rates decrease and the brain activity slows. After 90 minutes, they go from deep sleep to light, or REM (rapid-eye-movement), sleep. The eyes move under the eyelids and dreaming takes place. Breathing and heart rates increase, and brain activity increases. The body does not move, and the muscles are paralysed, probably to stop the sleeper from acting out his or her dreams. After five to ten minutes, a sleeper will return to deep sleep.

During the night this pattern is repeated up to five times, with REM sleep beginning about every 90 minutes. Deep sleep decreases during the night, and periods of REM sleep become longer, the final one lasting up to 50 minutes.

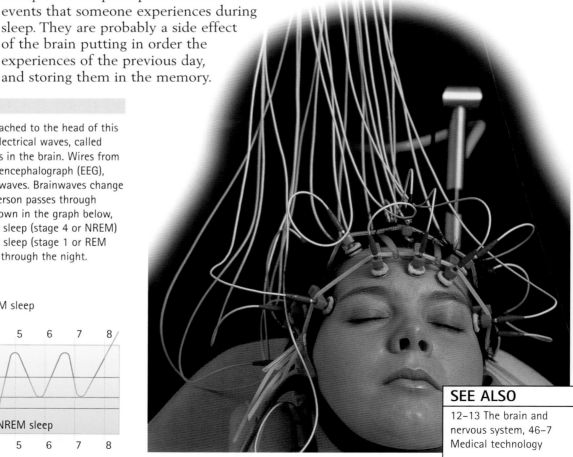

PATTERNS OF SLEEP

A number of electrodes are attached to the head of this sleeping woman. They detect electrical waves, called brainwaves, produced by nerves in the brain. Wires from the electrodes go to an electroencephalograph (EEG), which produces a trace of the waves. Brainwaves change during sleep, showing that a person passes through different stages of sleep. As shown in the graph below, the sleeper first goes into deep sleep (stage 4 or NREM) sleep, and then returns to light sleep (stage 1 or REM sleep). This pattern is repeated through the night.

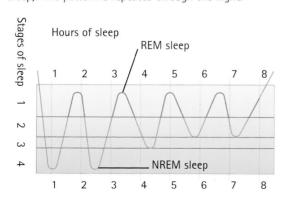

Stages of sleep

Hours of sleep

REM sleep

NREM sleep

SEE ALSO

12–13 The brain and nervous system, 46–7 Medical technology

COMMUNICATION

Communication plays an essential role for all animals. Humans are unique among animals in being able to use language to communicate with each other.

Vocal cord

Larynx

Trachea

During breathing, the vocal cords stay open to allow air in and out of the lungs.

Humans communicate in order to exchange thoughts, ideas or knowledge; to show friendship, indifference or aggression to others; or to reveal pleasure, anger or anxiety.

Communication takes various different forms. Body language involves positioning body parts, often without thinking, to convey a message. For example, facing someone and mimicking their body language usually indicates interest. Facial expressions, such as smiling, frowning, grimacing or pouting, are indicators of a person's mood and emotions.

LANGUAGE

Spoken language is unique to humans. Speech is controlled by an area on the left side of the brain. When a person wants to speak, nerve impulses are sent from here to muscles in the throat, mouth and jaw. Two flaps called vocal cords cross the larynx (voice box) and can open and close. Nerve messages from the brain cause larynx muscles to close and stretch the cords. Air from the lungs is then forced through the cords. The cords vibrate and produce sounds that pass into the throat, mouth and nose. Loose vocal cords produce low-pitched sounds; tight ones produce high-pitched sounds. Sounds are turned into speech by the position of the tongue, teeth and palate and the shape of the lips.

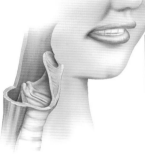

Air is forced through closed vocal cords to produce sounds during speech.

▲ At the top of the trachea is the larynx or voice box. Stretched across the larynx are two membranes called vocal cords. Normally these are open, but during speech they close. Air breathed out between closed cords makes them vibrate and produce sounds.

▶ Over 30 small muscles in the face produce a wide range of expressions. Most facial muscles are attached to a skull bone at one end and to the skin on the face at the other. When a facial muscle contracts, it pulls the skin to alter the appearance of the face. Facial expressions convey a person's moods and emotions and express a wide range of feelings from pleasure to anger.

▲ This frown is produced by the corrugator supercilii muscles.

Corrugator supercilii (pulls eyebrow down during frowning)

Masseter (closes jaw during eating)

Risorius (stretches mouth wide during laughing)

▼ To smile, the corners of the mouth are pulled up and out by the zygomaticus muscles.

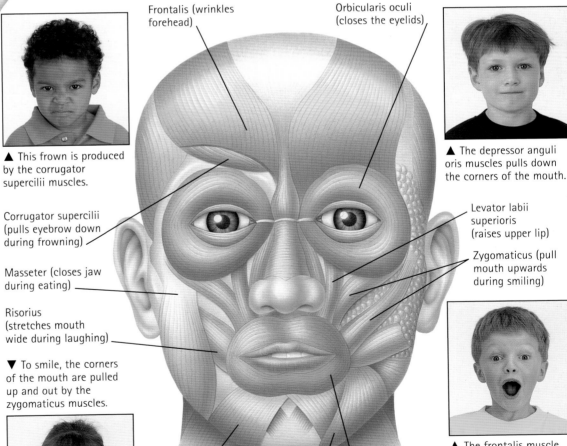

Frontalis (wrinkles forehead)

Orbicularis oculi (closes the eyelids)

▲ The depressor anguli oris muscles pulls down the corners of the mouth.

Levator labii superioris (raises upper lip)

Zygomaticus (pull mouth upwards during smiling)

▲ The frontalis muscle wrinkles the forehead and raises the eyebrows.

Orbicularis orisi (closes lips)

Depressor labii inferioris (pulls lower lip down)

Depressor anguli oris (turns corner of mouth downward)

SEE ALSO

10–11 Muscles and movement, 12–13 The brain and nervous system

TOUCH

The sense of touch provides the brain with information about the body's surroundings. Touch sensors are scattered all over the surface of the body.

This girl is blind but is able to read by running her fingertips across the page. The words are 'written' using the Braille system; its patterns of raised dots correspond to letters or numbers.

Sensors in the skin detect touch, pain, vibration, pressure, heat and cold. The softness of fur, the vibrations made by running the fingers over sandpaper, the pressure produced by holding a heavy weight, the pain of standing on a pin, the heat from a flame and the cold felt by plunging a hand into icy water – all of these are experienced when the skin's sensors are stimulated.

Sensors for light touch and pressure are in the upper part of the dermis of the skin. Those for heavy touch and pressure are larger and are found deeper in the dermis. Most of these sensors are enclosed in capsules. The sensors that detect heat, cold and pain are branched nerve endings near the junction between the epidermis and the dermis. These sensors are not enclosed in capsules. Information from all of the different sensors travels as electrical impulses along nerves that lead to the sensory area of the cerebrum (the main part of the brain). The brain interprets these impulses and provides a 'touch picture' of the person's surroundings, including information about pressure and warmth, for example. The feeling of pain warns the body about possible danger.

This boy looks strange because the size of his body parts have been drawn according to how sensitive to touch they are. Some parts of the body, such as fingers and lips, are much more sensitive than other parts because they have many more touch sensors.

HABITUATION
When a person dresses in the morning, the clothes can be felt as they are pulled over the skin. After a short while, the clothes can no longer be felt. This loss of feeling is called habituation. The skin gets used to the stimulation of the clothes, and nerve impulses are no longer sent to the brain. Habituation is important because without it clothes would irritate the skin all day.

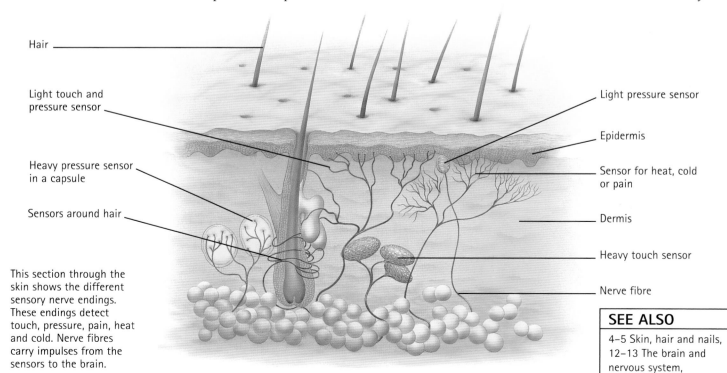

Hair

Light touch and pressure sensor

Heavy pressure sensor in a capsule

Sensors around hair

Light pressure sensor

Epidermis

Sensor for heat, cold or pain

Dermis

Heavy touch sensor

Nerve fibre

This section through the skin shows the different sensory nerve endings. These endings detect touch, pressure, pain, heat and cold. Nerve fibres carry impulses from the sensors to the brain.

SEE ALSO
4–5 Skin, hair and nails,
12–13 The brain and nervous system,
17 Taste and smell

TASTE AND SMELL

Taste and smell are linked senses. Both detect chemicals, either in food or in the air. Together, they enable people to appreciate a wide range of flavours.

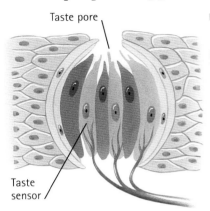

A mixture of taste sensors and packing cells are clustered together in this taste bud, similar to the segments of an orange. The taste bud detects chemicals dissolved in saliva that enter through the taste pore, which is the opening onto the tongue's surface.

The organ of taste is the tongue. Scattered over its upper surface are about 10,000 taste buds. Taste buds detect four basic tastes – sweet, sour, salty and bitter. Bitter-tasting foods may be poisonous and can be spat out.

Taste buds are found on the sides of tiny projections, called papillae, that cover the tongue. Fungiform papillae resemble mushrooms; seven or eight large ridged papillae are at the back of the tongue; threadlike filiform papillae lack taste buds and help to grip food during chewing. When dissolved food chemicals reach a taste bud, sensory cells send nerve impulses to the brain.

Taste buds occur in zones on the tongue: sweet at the front, bitter at the back and salty and sour along the sides. The tongue also has receptors for heat and cold and pain receptors for spicy foods.

A view magnified 180 times of the tongue's upper surface shows pointed filiform papillae surrounding a fungiform papilla (yellow-orange) in the sides of which are taste buds.

SMELL

The sense of smell enables people to enjoy food and avoid dangerous substances in the air and in food. Humans can detect over 10,000 different odours. About 10 million olfactory (smell) receptors are located in the upper part of the nasal cavity in two patches of epithelium (lining), each the size of a postage stamp. Each receptor contains up to 20 hair-like cilia. When air is breathed in, molecules dissolve in a watery mucus and bind to the cilia. Smell dominates taste; a heavy cold makes food flavourless.

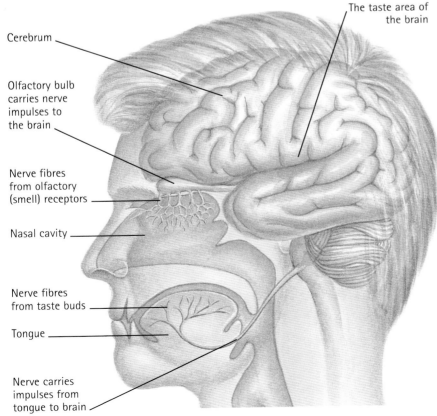

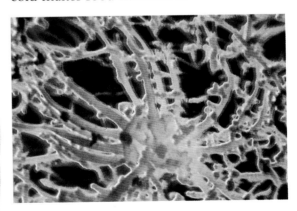

◀ Taste buds are found in the upper surface of the tongue. Impulses from taste buds travel along nerves to the taste area of the brain. Smell receptors are found in the upper part of each side of the nasal cavity. Nerve impulses from these receptors are sent to the part of the brain where smells are identified.

▲ Hair-like cilia (magnified 10,285 times) radiate from an olfactory (smell) receptor in the upper nasal cavity. When 'smelly' molecules touch these cilia, nerve impulses are sent to the brain.

SEE ALSO

12–13 The brain and nervous system, 18–19 Eyes and seeing, 20–1 Ears, hearing and balance

EYES AND SEEING

Vision is an extremely important sense. The eyes detect light from the body's surroundings and send messages to the brain, enabling a person to see.

The pupil is the hole that allows light into the eye. In dim light the coloured iris makes the pupil larger.

In bright light the iris makes the pupil smaller to prevent too much light entering the eye and damaging the retina.

Eyes are important because they provide the brain with much information about the body's surroundings. The retina, which lines the inside of the eye, contains photoreceptors, which are sensory cells that are stimulated by light. Photoreceptors make up 70 per cent of the sensory receptors in the human body, an indication of how important they are.

The two eyeballs, each about 2.5 cms in diameter, are found in orbits in the skull. Only a small part of the eye is visible from the front. Each eyeball moves using six extrinsic (external) muscles, which enable people to look from side to side and up and down. They cause tiny movements, saccades, of the eyeballs, that enable the eyes to constantly scan the surroundings.

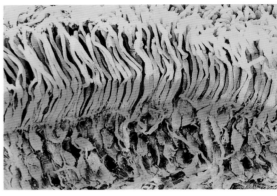

This is a section through the retina, the eye's light-sensitive layer. Rods and cones (yellow) respond to light and send messages to the brain along nerve fibres (pink).

BLIND SPOT

One region of the retina, known as the blind spot, does not contain any light sensors. This is where the optic nerve leaves the eyeball. The blind spot does not interfere with vision, however. Most of the time people do not notice any effect because the brain chooses to 'ignore' it.

THE EYE

The internal and external parts of the eye are revealed by this cutaway. Light enters through the clear cornea. The iris controls the amount of light that enters the eye so a person can see in both dim and bright light. The lens focuses light on the retina from both near and distant objects. The retina is packed with photoreceptors (light sensors).

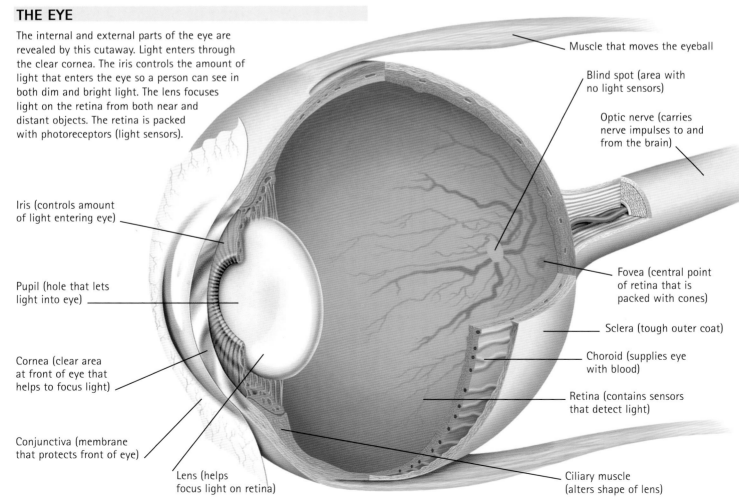

Muscle that moves the eyeball

Blind spot (area with no light sensors)

Optic nerve (carries nerve impulses to and from the brain)

Iris (controls amount of light entering eye)

Pupil (hole that lets light into eye)

Cornea (clear area at front of eye that helps to focus light)

Conjunctiva (membrane that protects front of eye)

Lens (helps focus light on retina)

Fovea (central point of retina that is packed with cones)

Sclera (tough outer coat)

Choroid (supplies eye with blood)

Retina (contains sensors that detect light)

Ciliary muscle (alters shape of lens)

HOW SIGHT WORKS

Light rays that enter the eye are refracted (bent) by the cornea and the lens to focus them on the retina. The ciliary muscle alters the thickness of the lens to focus light from near or distant objects. The iris controls the amount of light entering the eye. Its muscles continually alter the size of the pupil, making it large to admit more light or small to prevent excessive light from damaging the retina.

The retina is a thin layer of light sensors called rods and cones. The 120 million rods work best in dim light and are sensitive to black and white. About six million cones work best in bright light and detect colour. Cones are found mostly in the fovea, which generates the most detailed images. Three types of cone detect green, red and blue light, respectively. When they detect light, rods and cones generate nerve impulses that travel along the optic nerve to the visual areas at the back of the cerebrum, the main part of the brain. The brain reconstructs the images. Each eye detects a slightly different view. The brain uses these differences to produce a three-dimensional picture of the world that enables people to judge distances.

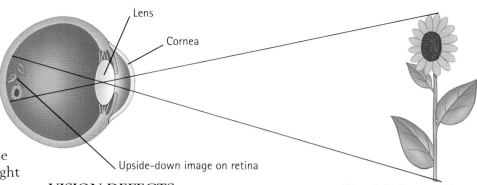

Lens

Cornea

Upside-down image on retina

VISION DEFECTS

Myopia, or short-sightedness, is an inability to see distant objects clearly because light from them is focused before it reaches the retina, producing a blurred image. This can be corrected by contact lenses or glasses. Hypermetropia, or long-sightedness, is an inability to see close objects clearly because light from them is focused 'behind' the retina, again producing a blurred image. This can be corrected by the use of glasses. Presbyopia may occur as part of ageing after the age of 45. Here, the ability to focus on near objects is lost, and glasses are needed for reading and other close-up work. Colour blindness, or colour deficiency, is the inability to distinguish between certain colours.

When light from an object enters the eye, the cornea and lens focus it to produce a clear, but upside-down, image on the retina. When hit by this light, sensors in the retina send nerve messages to the brain. There the image is 'seen' the right way up.

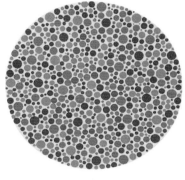

This pattern of dots is a test for colour blindness, an inability to tell certain colours apart. A colour-blind person lacks one of the types of cone (colour sensors) that detect red, green or blue light. Most common is red-green colour blindness, an inability to distinguish between those two colours. If you can see the number eight in this pattern, you are not colour blind. Colour blindness is more common in males than in females.

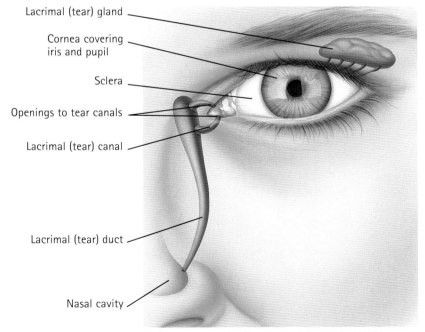

Lacrimal (tear) gland

Cornea covering iris and pupil

Sclera

Openings to tear canals

Lacrimal (tear) canal

Lacrimal (tear) duct

Nasal cavity

▲ Tears are produced by lacrimal (tear) glands. Tears spread over the eye's surface when a person blinks to wash away dirt and dust; they also contain the chemical lysozyme that kills bacteria. Tears then drain through two holes in the corner of the eye and empty into the nose.

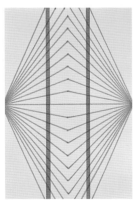
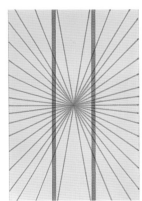

Optical illusions are images that trick the brain. Here both sets of red lines are straight, though they seem to curve inwards (left) or outwards (right).

SEE ALSO

12–13 The brain and nervous system, 16 Touch, 17 Taste and smell

EARS, HEARING AND BALANCE

Humans can detect over 400,000 different sounds. As well as detecting sound, the ears play an important role in balance and posture.

Sound is created by alternating waves of low and high pressure that pass through the air, similar to the ripples that spread across a pond when a stone is dropped into the water. These pressure waves pass into the ear where they are detected by sensors. These send messages to the brain, which interprets them as sounds.

Most of the ear lies hidden within the temporal bones of the skull. The part we can see, the pinna, channels sound waves into the auditory canal, a tube that secretes cleansing wax. The air-filled middle ear is bordered by the eardrum on one side and the oval window on the other. Its only opening is through the Eustachian, or auditory, tube that runs to the throat. It ensures that the air pressure on both sides of the eardrum is kept equal. If it is not, the eardrum cannot vibrate properly and hearing is impaired. Sudden pressure changes – such as when a train goes into a tunnel – can make the pressures unequal. Yawning or chewing forces air into, or out of, the Eustachian tube from the throat, and the ears 'pop' as the pressures equalize and normal hearing returns. The inner ear contains sound receptors and links to the brain. It is filled with fluid and sealed in a bony structure.

HOW HEARING WORKS

Sound waves arrive from the source that is making them, such as a radio, and enter the ear through the auditory canal. At the end of this canal, a taut piece of skin called the eardrum vibrates as the sound waves hit it. The eardrum passes on the vibrations to the three ossicles – the hammer, anvil and stirrup – in the middle ear. When these bones vibrate, the stirrup bone pushes and pulls the membrane that covers the oval window. This movement sets up vibrations in the fluid in the inner ear, which are detected by the sensors in the cochlea. The sensors send nerve impulses to the brain, which processes them. The person hears the sound. Loud sounds cause bigger vibrations in the fluid. The part of the cochlea near the oval window detects high-pitched sounds, while the tip of the cochlea's coil detects low-pitched sounds.

Sound waves usually arrive in one ear a split second before the other. The brain uses this tiny time difference to work out from which direction the sound came.

INSIDE THE EAR

The outer ear channels sounds into the ear. The middle ear is crossed by three tiny bones, called ossicles, that transmit sounds from the eardrum to the inner ear. The inner ear is filled with fluid and a series of channels. The cochlea contains sound sensors. The semicircular canals, and the saccule and the utricle, detect movement and position.

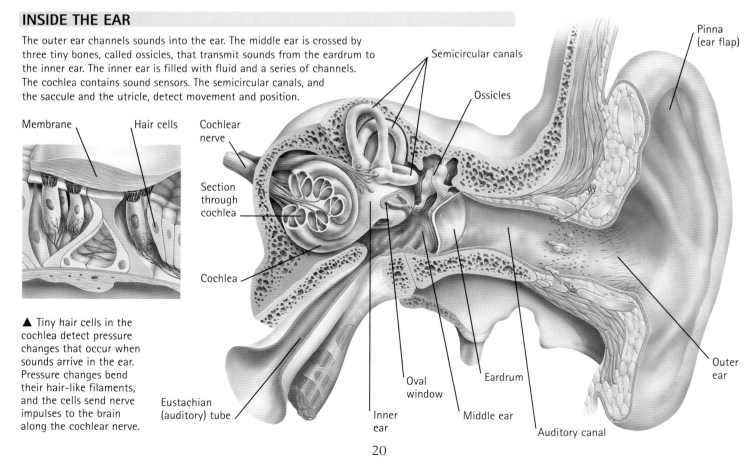

Membrane   Hair cells   Cochlear nerve

Section through cochlea

Cochlea

▲ Tiny hair cells in the cochlea detect pressure changes that occur when sounds arrive in the ear. Pressure changes bend their hair-like filaments, and the cells send nerve impulses to the brain along the cochlear nerve.

Eustachian (auditory) tube

Semicircular canals

Ossicles

Pinna (ear flap)

Oval window

Inner ear

Eardrum

Middle ear

Outer ear

Auditory canal

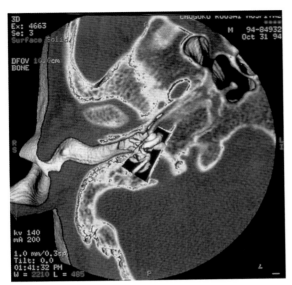

This CT scan shows a section through a living ear. The ear canal (white) runs from the left to the centre. The ear bones – ossicles – are highlighted in the centre. The larger grey, mottled areas are the bones of the skull.

This view (magnified 2,074 times) of the inner ear shows the region of the cochlea that detects sounds. When sounds arrive and cause vibrations in the fluid, the filaments of the hair cells (yellow and V-shaped) bend, and the hair cells send messages to the brain.

THE EARS AND BALANCE

Balance sensors are found within the inner ear inside two linked structures – the semicircular canals and the vestibule. These lie next to the cochlea and are also filled with fluid. The three semicircular canals are set at right angles to each other and detect movements of the head. At the base of each canal, sensory hair cells are embedded in a jelly-like cupule (cup-shaped structure). When the head moves, the fluid in one or more of the canals moves and bends both the cupule and its hairs. The hair cells then send nerve impulses to the brain. By analysing which semicircular canals sent nerve messages, the brain can tell which way the head and body are moving at any moment.

The vestibule contains two balance sensors, the utricle and the saccule. Both contain sensory hairs embedded in otoliths (ear parts made of calcium carbonate crystals). The utricle detects rapid acceleration and deceleration, while the saccule detects changes in the head's position. This information is combined with messages from the eyes, pressure sensors in the feet and receptors in muscles and joints to provide the brain with a complete picture of the body's position. The brain can then send out instructions to muscles to alter the body's position to maintain its posture and balance.

HEARING RANGES

Humans can hear a wide range of sounds, from low-pitched hums to high-pitched squeaks. Pitch is determined by a sound's frequency; that is, how rapidly one crest of the wave follows the previous one. Sound frequency is measured in hertz (Hz), or sound waves per second.

Young people can usually hear sounds between 20 Hz and 20,000 Hz. However, the range of sounds people can hear decreases with their age, so older people are unable to hear higher-pitched sounds. Some mammals hear high-pitched sounds that are inaudible to humans. Bats can hear sounds in the range 1,000 to 120,000 Hz, and cats from 60 to 65,000 Hz.

▲ The semicircular canals, and the utricle and the saccule play an important part in balance. They send information to the brain about the position and movement of the head. The brain instructs muscles to move and position the body so that it does not fall over.

◄ Inside each fluid-filled semicircular canal is a jelly-like knob called a cupule. Embedded in the cupule are hair cells. If the head moves, the fluid also moves and bends the cupule. Hair cells send messages to the brain so that a person is aware of their movement.

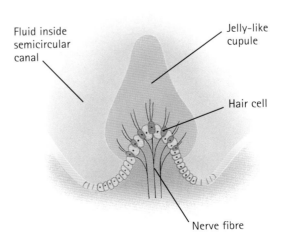

Fluid inside semicircular canal

Jelly-like cupule

Hair cell

Nerve fibre

SEE ALSO

10–11 Muscles and movement, 12–13 The brain and nervous system

HORMONES

The endocrine system releases chemical messengers called hormones into the body. Different hormones control processes such as reproduction and growth.

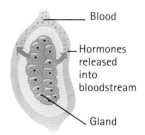

- Blood
- Hormones released into bloodstream
- Gland

A gland is a group of cells that releases chemicals either into or onto the body. Endocrine, or ductless, glands (above) release hormones into the bloodstream. The blood carries them to the part of the body where they have their effect.

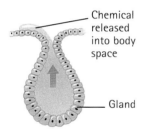

- Chemical released into body space
- Gland

Exocrine glands include the salivary glands and sweat glands. Also called ducted glands, exocrine glands release their secretions, such as saliva or sweat, through a duct that opens into a space inside the body or onto the surface of the body.

The endocrine, or hormonal, system is made up of a number of endocrine (hormone-releasing) glands. Along with the nervous system, the endocrine system controls and coordinates the workings of the body. The endocrine system plays a key role in reproduction and growth and controls many other processes. The endocrine and nervous systems work in very different ways. In the nervous system, messages are carried in the form of electrical impulses. The endocrine system releases chemical messengers, called hormones, into the bloodstream. Carried by the blood to its target, the hormone alters the activities of cells by increasing or decreasing the speed of processes taking place inside them. Unlike the nervous system, hormones work slowly and have long-term effects. The pituitary gland controls most of the other endocrine glands. In turn, the pituitary gland is controlled by the hypothalamus in the brain. This provides a direct link between the endocrine and nervous systems.

THE ENDOCRINE SYSTEM

The glands that make up the endocrine system are scattered through the head, thorax and abdomen. The major endocrine glands are the pituitary, thyroid, parathyroid and adrenal glands. The pituitary gland releases more than nine hormones, controls the activities of most other endocrine glands and is itself controlled by part of the brain called the hypothalamus. The thyroid gland regulates the body's metabolic rate (the speed of chemical reactions inside body cells). Along with the parathyroid glands, it also controls calcium levels in the blood. The adrenal glands also affect metabolic rate and help the body withstand stress. Other organs also have endocrine sections. The pancreas controls glucose levels in the blood, but it also acts as an exocrine gland that releases digestive enzymes into the intestine. The testes in males and the ovaries in females produce sex hormones as well as making sperm and eggs.

REGULATING HORMONES

Hormone levels in the blood are regulated by negative feedback systems. These reverse unwanted changes, ensuring that hormones do not have too great or too little an effect. For example, thyroxine speeds up the body's metabolism. Too much thyroxine, and the body works too fast. Too little, and the body slows right down. Low thyroxine levels cause the pituitary gland to release thyroid stimulating hormone (TSH), and the thyroid gland produces thyroxine. High thyroxine levels have the opposite effect.

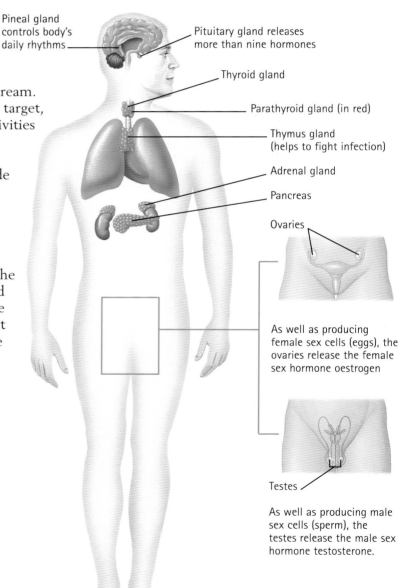

Pineal gland controls body's daily rhythms

Pituitary gland releases more than nine hormones

Thyroid gland

Parathyroid gland (in red)

Thymus gland (helps to fight infection)

Adrenal gland

Pancreas

Ovaries

As well as producing female sex cells (eggs), the ovaries release the female sex hormone oestrogen

Testes

As well as producing male sex cells (sperm), the testes release the male sex hormone testosterone.

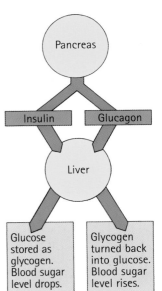

The passengers on this roller coaster ride are experiencing the effects of the hormone adrenaline. Adrenaline is released by the adrenal glands. It helps the body to deal with dangerous situations. Adrenaline makes the heart beat and breathing faster. It also diverts blood to the muscles. Following the release of adrenaline the body is prepared to either confront dangerous situations or run away from them, a reaction called fight-or-flight.

PITUITARY GLAND

The pea-sized pituitary gland at the base of the brain helps to control the endocrine system. The pituitary gland releases more than nine hormones. Some control body functions directly, such as a growth hormone that stimulates growth. Others target other endocrine glands, such as follicle stimulating hormone that stimulates the ovaries to release the female sex hormone oestrogen.

The pituitary gland is made up of two parts called lobes. The larger anterior (front) lobe makes and releases most pituitary hormones. Their release is triggered by hormones secreted by the hypothalamus in the base of the brain. The smaller posterior (back) lobe stores and releases two hormones made by the hypothalamus.

ADRENAL GLANDS

The adrenal glands sit at the top of each kidney. The outer cortex of these glands releases hormones called corticosteroids, that help to control metabolism and regulate the concentration of substances in the blood. The inner medulla secretes adrenaline. If the brain perceives danger or stress, it sends nerve messages to the adrenal glands, causing them to secrete adrenaline. This prepares the body to confront the threat or run away from it.

PANCREAS

The pancreas is located below the stomach. It releases the hormones insulin and glucagon, which control blood glucose levels. Cells need a constant supply of glucose. If glucose levels are too high or too low, cells cannot take glucose in. Insulin and glucagon naturally balance each other to maintain a steady glucose level whether a person is hungry or has just eaten.

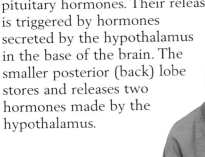

Every day this boy uses a special automatic syringe to inject insulin into his body. He suffers from diabetes, which means his pancreas does not produce insulin. Without the injections, the boy's body cannot control glucose levels in the blood and he would become very ill.

The pancreas releases insulin and glucagon. These hormones work in opposite ways to regulate levels of glucose in the bloodstream. If glucose levels rise, the insulin stimulates cells to take up glucose and the liver to store it as glycogen. If glucose levels fall, glucagon stimulates the liver to turn glycogen back into glucose.

SEE ALSO

12–13 The brain and nervous system, 26 Blood, 34 Metabolism, 36 Reproduction

HEART AND CIRCULATION

The circulatory system supplies the body's cells with all their needs. It consists of the heart, the blood vessels and blood that flows through them.

English doctor William Harvey (1578-1657) was the first person to show that blood circulates in one direction around the body, pumped by the heart.

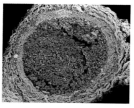

The magnified cross-section above shows the thick walls of an artery.

The heart pumps blood through a network of blood vessels, which extend 150,000 kilometres around the human body. There are three main types of blood vessels. Thick-walled arteries carry blood away from the heart. Thinner-walled veins carry blood back to the heart. Microscopic capillaries link veins and arteries. Formed as branches of arterioles (the smallest arteries), capillaries pass through tissues and supply groups of cells with essential substances. Waste products flow back into the capillaries. Capillaries link up to form venules, which unite to form veins. The human circulatory system is a double circulation with two 'loops'. One loop carries blood to the lungs. The other carries blood to the body. It takes blood about 60 seconds to complete a full circuit of the body.

ANATOMY OF THE HEART

The heart is a powerful, muscular pump that maintains a continuous flow of blood around the body. The heart is divided into two halves by the septum. Each half has a smaller upper chamber, called the atrium, and a larger lower chamber, called the ventricle. The right atrium receives oxygen-poor blood from the body through large veins called the superior (upper) vena cava and inferior (lower) vena cava. The pulmonary arteries carry blood pumped from the right ventricle to the lungs. The left atrium receives oxygen-rich blood from the lungs through the pulmonary veins. The left ventricle pumps the oxygen-rich blood to the body's cells along a large artery called the aorta.

◄ Blood flows from the arteries along tiny capillaries, which supply cells, to the veins

Labels: Arteriole, Venule, Capillary, Artery, Vein

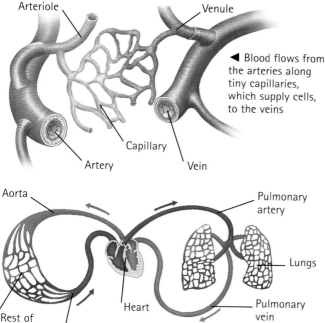

Labels: Aorta, Pulmonary artery, Lungs, Pulmonary vein, Heart, Vena cava, Rest of body

▲ The circulatory system is made up of two 'loops'. One carries oxygen-poor blood from the heart to the lungs (where it picks up oxygen) and back to the heart. The other carries oxygen-rich blood from the heart to the rest of the body (where it supplies oxygen to all body tissues) and then back to the heart.

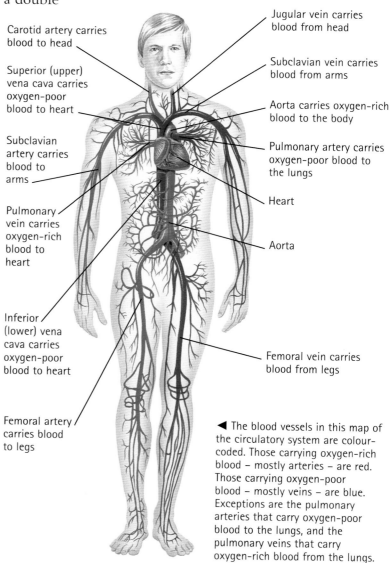

Labels: Carotid artery carries blood to head; Superior (upper) vena cava carries oxygen-poor blood to heart; Subclavian artery carries blood to arms; Pulmonary vein carries oxygen-rich blood to heart; Inferior (lower) vena cava carries oxygen-poor blood to heart; Femoral artery carries blood to legs; Jugular vein carries blood from head; Subclavian vein carries blood from arms; Aorta carries oxygen-rich blood to the body; Pulmonary artery carries oxygen-poor blood to the lungs; Heart; Aorta; Femoral vein carries blood from legs

◄ The blood vessels in this map of the circulatory system are colour-coded. Those carrying oxygen-rich blood – mostly arteries – are red. Those carrying oxygen-poor blood – mostly veins – are blue. Exceptions are the pulmonary arteries that carry oxygen-poor blood to the lungs, and the pulmonary veins that carry oxygen-rich blood from the lungs.

THE HEART

The front view of the heart (below) shows the main blood vessels carrying blood to and from the heart and the coronary artery that supplies the heart wall. A section through the heart (below right) shows the septum that divides the heart into left and right halves, the atria and the larger ventricles. Heart valves prevent blood flowing backwards.

Superior vena cava

Aorta

Pulmonary artery

Pulmonary veins

Left atrium

Right atrium

Left ventricle

Inferior vena cava

Right ventricle

Coronary artery

Right atrium

Aorta

Semilunar valve guarding exit into pulmonary artery

Left atrium

Bicuspid valve between left atrium and left ventricle

Left ventricle

Tricuspid valve between right atrium and right ventricle

Septum

Right ventricle

Thick muscular wall

CORONARY CIRCULATION

Blood passes through the heart too quickly to supply the muscle cells in the heart wall with the oxygen and food they need. The heart has its own blood supply called the coronary circulation. Two coronary arteries branch from the aorta and supply all parts of the heart wall. Blood that has passed through heart muscle empties into the right atrium. If a coronary artery becomes blocked, the part of the heart it supplies may die and cause a heart attack.

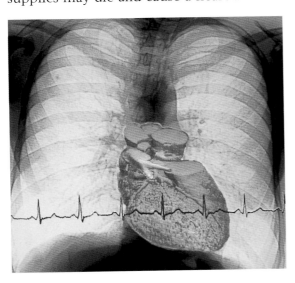

HEARTBEAT

During a single heartbeat, both ventricles fill with blood and then contract to pump blood out of the heart. As the heart fills with blood, semilunar valves close to prevent backflow into the heart from the aorta and pulmonary artery. As the heart empties, valves between the atria and ventricles close to prevent blood flowing back into the atria. As the valves between atria and ventricles close, they produce a long 'lubb' sound. As the semilunar valves close, they produce a shorter 'dupp' sound. Together, these sounds make up the heartbeat, which can be heard using an instrument called a stethoscope. The timing of each heartbeat is regulated by a 'pacemaker' in the wall of the right atrium.

▶ On average, the heart beats about 75 times a minute. Each heartbeat is a cycle of three stages – diastole, atrial systole and ventricular systole. These stages follow each other in a precisely timed sequence. Over the course of the three stages blood enters the atria, passes into the ventricles and is then pumped out of the heart.

◀ This X-ray shows the heart located inside the thorax (chest) between the two lungs (yellow). The ribs, also visible, surround and protect both heart and lungs. Also shown is an electrocardiograph (ECG), which is a record of the electrical changes taking place in the heart.

During diastole, the atria and ventricles are relaxed. Both atria fill with blood.

During atrial systole, the atria contract and squeeze blood into the ventricles.

During ventricular systole, the ventricles contract and push blood from the heart.

SEE ALSO

26 Blood, 27 Lymphatic system, 28–9 Lungs and breathing, 34 Metabolism

BLOOD

Blood provides the body's trillions of cells with a delivery and removal system. It also helps to defend the body against infection and repairs damaged blood cells.

▲ Red blood cells, white blood cells (yellow) and platelets (pink) are made in bone marrow. About two million red blood cells are produced every second.

Red blood cells caught in platelet net

Damage to a blood vessel causes the platelets to form a 'net' of fibres that traps red blood cells.

Scab forms

Fibres and red blood cells form a clot to seal off the wound. The surface of the clot hardens into a scab.

Healed tissue under old scab

Underneath the scab, the blood vessel and skin repair themselves. Once this is done, the old, dried-up scab falls off.

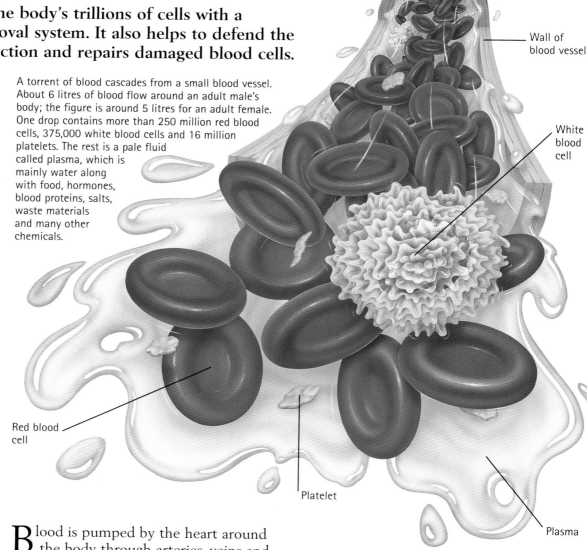

A torrent of blood cascades from a small blood vessel. About 6 litres of blood flow around an adult male's body; the figure is around 5 litres for an adult female. One drop contains more than 250 million red blood cells, 375,000 white blood cells and 16 million platelets. The rest is a pale fluid called plasma, which is mainly water along with food, hormones, blood proteins, salts, waste materials and many other chemicals.

Wall of blood vessel

White blood cell

Red blood cell

Platelet

Plasma

Blood is pumped by the heart around the body through arteries, veins and capillaries. It supplies food and oxygen to the body's cells and removes wastes. Blood also maintains the body's temperature, fights disease and plays a role in repairing damaged blood vessels.

BLOOD AS A TRANSPORT SYSTEM

Oxygen is transported to cells by doughnut-shaped red blood cells. These are packed with haemoglobin, a substance that picks up oxygen as blood passes through the lungs and releases it into the body's cells. Plasma is a watery liquid that makes up about 55 per cent of blood. It is responsible for transporting food, waste products, chemical messengers called hormones and many other substances around the body. It also helps the body to maintain a temperature of around 37°C.

DEFENCE AND PROTECTION

Tiny disease-causing micro-organisms (pathogens) are constantly trying to infect the human body. White blood cells called phagocytes and lymphocytes destroy these invaders. Phagocytes hunt down and engulf any pathogens. Lymphocytes release killer chemicals called antibodies. These disable pathogens so that phagocytes can engulf them. Lymphocytes remember pathogens so that they can react even faster if the same pathogens invade again.

Platelets seal leaks in damaged blood vessels. Their action stops pathogens from getting into the body and also prevents the loss of blood from the damaged area.

SEE ALSO

24–5 Heart and circulation, 41 The immune system

26

LYMPHATIC SYSTEM

The lymphatic system is a transport system that drains fluid called lymph from the tissues into the blood. It also contains cells that defend the body against disease.

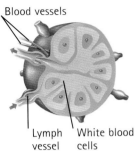

Blood vessels

Lymph vessel   White blood cells

▲ A lymph node is a mass of white blood cells and a network of fibres. Debris and pathogens are removed from lymph as it passes through the node.

A s blood flows along the circulatory system, a substance called tissue fluid passes out through the capillary walls. This fluid delivers oxygen and essential nutrients to tissue cells. Tissue fluid then removes wastes and returns back into the bloodstream through the capillary walls.

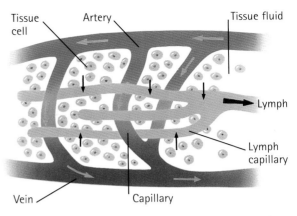

Tissue cell   Artery   Tissue fluid

Lymph

Lymph capillary

Vein   Capillary

Cells in the body's tissues are bathed in a fluid derived from nearby blood capillaries. Excess tissue fluid passes into blind-ending lymph capillaries and becomes lymph.

DRAINAGE
Every day, about 24 litres of fluid leaves the capillaries that pass through the tissues. Most returns directly back to the blood, but about 4 litres remains. The lymphatic system drains the excess fluid, now called lymph, and empties it back into the blood vessels in the upper chest.

Lymph is a colourless fluid that contains dissolved substances, debris and pathogens such as bacteria and viruses. It only flows in one direction – away from the tissues. Unlike blood, which has a heart to pump it, lymph moves through the lymphatic system with the help of skeletal muscles that push the fluid along when they contract. Valves in the lymph vessels stop the fluid flowing backwards.

DEFENCE
As lymph flows through lymph vessels, it passes through lymph nodes. Here, white blood cells called macrophages trap and engulf cell debris and pathogens. Other white blood cells, called lymphocytes, produce antibodies which are chemicals that mark pathogens for destruction. Other lymphatic organs have a similar role. The tonsils intercept pathogens that enter the mouth. Together, lymphocytes and macrophages form the immune system, the body's most powerful defence against disease.

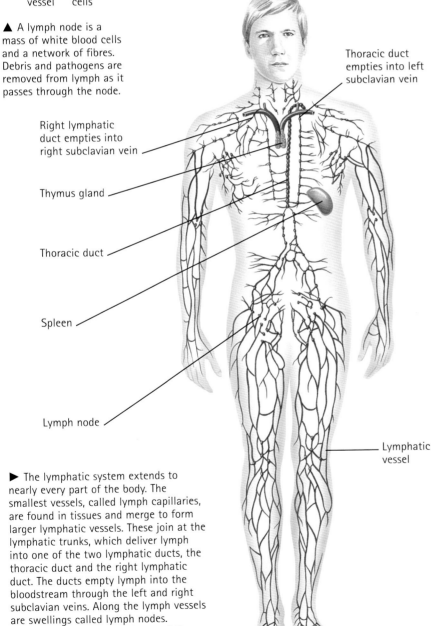

Thoracic duct empties into left subclavian vein

Right lymphatic duct empties into right subclavian vein

Thymus gland

Thoracic duct

Spleen

Lymph node

Lymphatic vessel

► The lymphatic system extends to nearly every part of the body. The smallest vessels, called lymph capillaries, are found in tissues and merge to form larger lymphatic vessels. These join at the lymphatic trunks, which deliver lymph into one of the two lymphatic ducts, the thoracic duct and the right lymphatic duct. The ducts empty lymph into the bloodstream through the left and right subclavian veins. Along the lymph vessels are swellings called lymph nodes. The spleen is an important part of the lymphatic system and is a primary filter for the blood. It also makes antibodies.

SEE ALSO

2–3 Body organization, 24–5 Heart and circulation, 41 The immune system

LUNGS AND BREATHING

Humans need oxygen to live. It is obtained from air breathed into the lungs. In the lungs, oxygen passes into the bloodstream and is then carried to the body's cells.

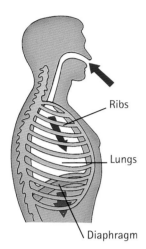

During inhalation, or the process of breathing in, the diaphragm contracts and flattens. The intercostal muscles also contract and pull the ribs upwards and outwards. This makes the lungs bigger and decreases the pressure inside them so that air is sucked into them through the mouth and trachea.

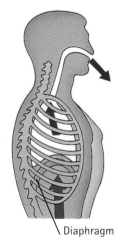

During exhalation, or the process of breathing out, the diaphragm relaxes and is pushed up by the abdominal organs beneath it. The intercostal muscles relax, so the ribs move downwards and inwards. This decreases volume inside the thorax. The lungs get smaller and pressure inside increases so that air is pushed out.

Cells need a constant supply of energy to power their activities. Cells use oxygen to release energy from foods in a process called respiration. Respiration releases carbon dioxide, a poisonous waste product which must be removed from the body. Delivering oxygen and removing carbon dioxide is done by the respiratory system. This consists of a system of tubes that carry air in and out of the body, and a pair of lungs through which oxygen enters, and carbon dioxide leaves, the blood. Blood carries oxygen from the lungs to the cells, and transports waste carbon dioxide from the cells back to the lungs.

A SYSTEM OF TUBES

Air first passes through the nose. Hairs in the nostrils and sticky mucus lining the nasal cavity trap particles that would damage the lungs. Air then passes into the pharynx, through the larynx (voice box) into the trachea, which is reinforced by C-shaped pieces of cartilage. Mucus in the trachea also traps dirt. Fine hair-like cilia carry dirt up to the throat. The trachea branches into two bronchi, which themselves branch inside the lungs.

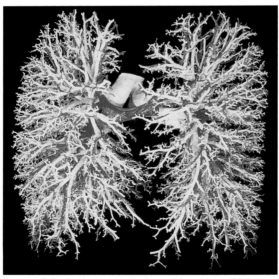

A cast of the lungs shows the bronchi and bronchioles (white) and the pulmonary artery (red). This network is called the bronchial tree – it resembles an upside-down tree with the trachea as trunk and bronchi as branches.

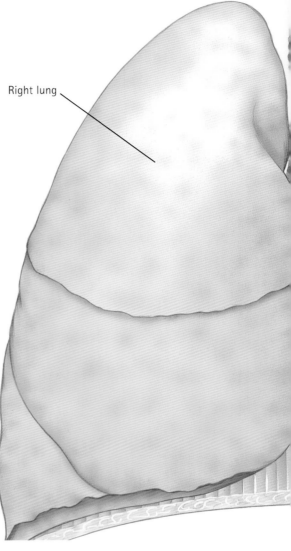

THE LUNGS

The lungs lie in the thorax (chest) and sit either side of the heart, protected by the backbone and ribcage. They rest on the diaphragm, a muscular sheet that separates the thorax from the abdomen. Healthy lungs are pink because they are full of blood. They also feel spongy, because they consist of a branching network of airways that end in millions of microscopic air sacs called alveoli, through which oxygen enters the bloodstream. Squeezed into the chest, all the alveoli provide a surface area for absorbing oxygen equivalent to two-thirds that of a tennis court. A thin pleural membrane covers the lungs; another lines the inside of the chest wall. Fluid between the membranes decreases friction and prevents pain during breathing.

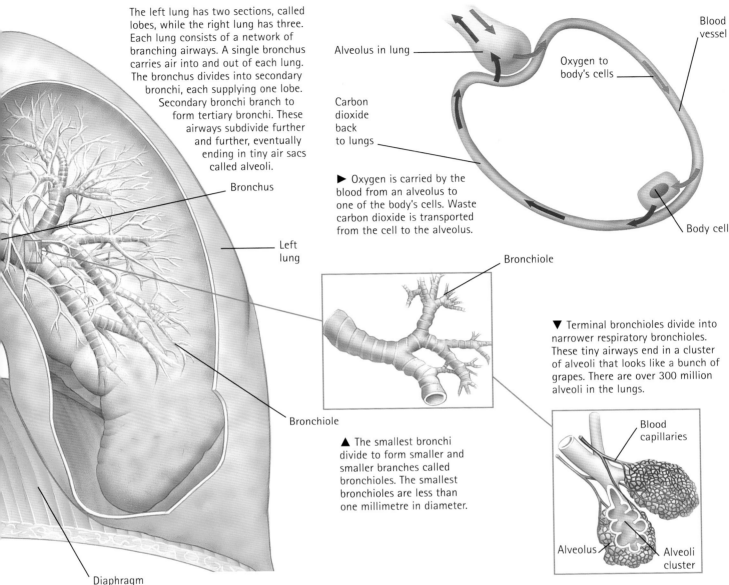

The left lung has two sections, called lobes, while the right lung has three. Each lung consists of a network of branching airways. A single bronchus carries air into and out of each lung. The bronchus divides into secondary bronchi, each supplying one lobe. Secondary bronchi branch to form tertiary bronchi. These airways subdivide further and further, eventually ending in tiny air sacs called alveoli.

Bronchus

Left lung

Diaphragm

Alveolus in lung

Carbon dioxide back to lungs

Oxygen to body's cells

Blood vessel

Body cell

▶ Oxygen is carried by the blood from an alveolus to one of the body's cells. Waste carbon dioxide is transported from the cell to the alveolus.

Bronchiole

Bronchiole

▼ Terminal bronchioles divide into narrower respiratory bronchioles. These tiny airways end in a cluster of alveoli that looks like a bunch of grapes. There are over 300 million alveoli in the lungs.

▲ The smallest bronchi divide to form smaller and smaller branches called bronchioles. The smallest bronchioles are less than one millimetre in diameter.

Blood capillaries

Alveolus

Alveoli cluster

GAS EXCHANGE

Gas exchange takes place continuously in the alveoli. This process ensures that the body's cells receive a constant supply of oxygen and are not poisoned by the accumulation of carbon dioxide. Oxygen dissolves in a thin layer of liquid that lines each alveolus, then moves by diffusion – the movement of molecules from a high concentration to a low concentration – across the thin wall of the alveolus into the blood capillary and into red blood cells. Carbon dioxide diffuses in the reverse direction from the blood into the air inside the alveolus and is exhaled. Inhaled air contains about 21 per cent oxygen and 0.04 per cent carbon dioxide. Exhaled air contains 16 per cent oxygen and about 4 per cent carbon dioxide.

BREATHING

Breathing, or ventilation, moves fresh air into the lungs to replenish supplies of oxygen. It also forces stale air out of the lungs to remove carbon dioxide. The elastic lungs depend on the diaphragm and rib muscles to change the shape of the thorax. Pleural membranes cover the lungs' surfaces and line the chest wall. They act like an 'adhesive pad', ensuring that the lungs follow the movement of the thorax. During inhalation, the diaphragm and intercostal muscles between the ribs contract. This makes the thorax and the lungs larger – and the pressure inside them lower – so that air is sucked in. During exhalation, the reverse occurs. The lungs never completely fill or empty – a reservoir of air remains and is refreshed.

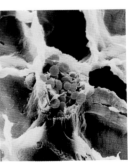

A view inside the lung magnified 410 times reveals a blood capillary filled with red blood cells. These cells pick up oxygen from the surrounding network of alveoli.

SEE ALSO
24–5 Heart and circulation, 26 Blood, 35 Waste disposal

FOOD AND NUTRITION

Food provides the body with vital substances called nutrients. Good nutrition means that the body has an adequate, balanced supply of nutrients.

The process by which humans obtain a regular supply of food to survive is called nutrition. Most food contains a variety of nutrients, which are released during digestion. Macronutrients – carbohydrates, proteins and fats – are needed in large amounts each day. Carbohydrates provide energy. They include complex starches found in potatoes and pasta and simple sugars in fruits and sweets. Proteins provide simple building blocks called amino acids for growth and repair. Fats provide energy and help insulate the body. Micronutrients – vitamins and minerals – are only needed in tiny amounts daily but are essential for cells to function. They include vitamins such as vitamins A and C, and minerals such as calcium. Also essential are water to maintain the body's fluid balance, and fibre, undigested plant material that keeps the intestinal muscles working properly.

A person who regularly eats fast food is not likely to be receiving a balanced diet. Although the meal shown above contains some carbohydrate in the bun and french fries, it is also very rich in protein and animal fats. It contains no fruit or fresh vegetables to provide vitamins or minerals.

Meals should be well balanced. Pasta and bread provide carbohydrate; beans and fish supply protein and vitamins with some fat; salad contains vitamins, minerals and fibre.

BALANCED DIET

The word *diet* refers to the type and amount of food a person eats each day. To maintain good health and avoid weight gain, a person's diet should be balanced, containing a range of nutrients in the right amounts. A balanced diet consists of about 50 per cent carbohydrates (mostly complex starches), about 20 per cent protein, 15 per cent or less fat (unsaturated fats from plant oils and oily fish are healthier than saturated fats from meat or dairy products) and 15 per cent fibre. It should also include plenty of fresh fruit and vegetables.

THE FOOD PYRAMID

The food pyramid provides an easy way to plan a balanced diet. The bulk of a balanced diet should be made up of starchy, carbohydrate-rich foods, along with smaller amounts of proteins and fats (preferably not animal fats). It should also provide plenty of vitamins, minerals and fibre. The food pyramid provides a simple way of getting the balance right by showing the proportions in which the main types of foods should be eaten. Starchy foods, such as rice and bread, and vitamin-, mineral- and fibre-rich foods, such as vegetables and fruits, are found towards the base of the pyramid. Those that should be eaten in smaller amounts, such as meat and dairy products, are further up the pyramid. Those that should be eaten sparingly or not at all, such as sugary cakes and sweets, are located at the narrow top of the food pyramid.

Foods rich in fat and sugar should only be eaten in small amounts.

Foods rich in protein such as beans, fish, chicken, meat and cheese. Protein is essential for growth and tissue repair. Meat and cheese also contain a lot of fat.

Fresh fruit and vegetables provide vitamins and minerals that are essential for good health and fibre (roughage) that keeps the digestive system working properly.

Foods rich in starchy carbohydrates such as rice, bread, potatoes and pasta. Such foods release energy slowly throughout the day.

SEE ALSO

32–3 Digestion, 34 Metabolism, 35 Waste disposal

TEETH

Teeth perform an important role at the start of digestion. They grip food, chop it into small pieces and crush it so that it can be swallowed with saliva.

A view magnified 4,958 times of bacteria living on a human tooth. Unless teeth are cleaned regularly, these bacteria form a hard coating called plaque. The bacteria in plaque feed on sugars and release acids that eat into the tooth and cause decay.

Teeth are hard structures that emerge from soft gums and are firmly set in the upper and lower jaws. Each tooth consists of an upper, visible crown and a lower, hidden root. The 32 teeth in an adult's mouth vary in shape and function. In each jaw four chisel-shaped incisors grip and chop food, two pointed canines pierce and tear food and four flattened premolars, along with six large molars, crush and grind food.

Humans have two sets of teeth during their lifetime. The first set of 20 milk, or deciduous, teeth erupt (appear) between the ages of 6 and 30 months. The second set of 32 adult, or permanent, teeth are already in place in the gums. From the age of six, the permanent teeth gradually erupt, replacing the milk teeth, which fall out. The last permanent teeth to appear, the back molars, or wisdom teeth, usually do so during the teenage years.

CHEWING AND SWALLOWING

The lips and front teeth pull food inside the mouth. Powerful muscles move the lower jaw up and down to crush food between the premolar and molar teeth. Three pairs of salivary glands squirt saliva into the mouth, and the tongue mixes the ground-up food with the saliva. The tongue pushes the slippery 'package' of food, called a bolus, into the throat. The bolus sets off an automatic reflex action of muscular contraction, called peristalsis. This pushes chewed food towards the stomach for the next part of digestion.

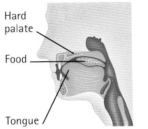
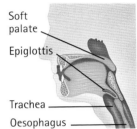

Hard palate

Food

Tongue

Soft palate

Epiglottis

Trachea

Oesophagus

▲ The tongue pushes food into the throat. The reflex action of peristalsis squeezes food down the oesophagus. The epiglottis closes off the opening to the windpipe to prevent food from entering the lungs.

STRUCTURE OF TEETH

Teeth are made up of several layers. The outer layer covers the crown and is made of enamel, the hardest material in the body. Dentine is a bone-like material that forms roots in the jawbone. The soft pulp cavity contains blood vessels to keep the tooth alive and nerve fibres that enable a person to feel when they are chewing.

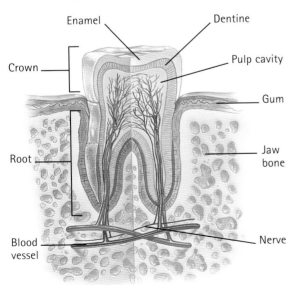

Enamel

Dentine

Crown

Pulp cavity

Gum

Jaw bone

Root

Blood vessel

Nerve

▶ Milk teeth are pushed out and replaced by adult teeth from the jaw below them.

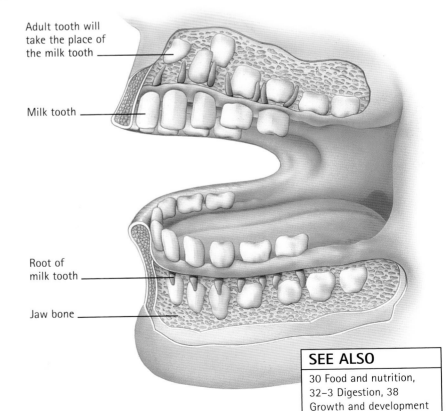

Adult tooth will take the place of the milk tooth

Milk tooth

Root of milk tooth

Jaw bone

SEE ALSO

30 Food and nutrition, 32–3 Digestion, 38 Growth and development

DIGESTION

The digestion of food releases simple nutrients in a form that can be used by the body's cells. This process takes place in the digestive system.

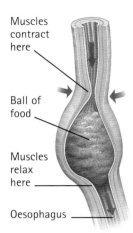

Muscles contract here

Ball of food

Muscles relax here

Oesophagus

Swallowed food is pushed down the oesophagus by wave-like muscular contractions called peristalsis. The muscles contract behind the food to push it downwards.

The nutrients essential for life are 'locked' inside the large molecules that make up food. The job of the digestive system is to break down these large molecules – such as carbohydrates, proteins and fats – to release simple nutrients such as sugars, amino acids and fatty acids.

The digestive process has four stages: ingestion, digestion, absorption and egestion. During ingestion, the food is taken into the mouth, chewed and swallowed. During digestion, food is broken down either by muscular crushing or by chemicals called enzymes. Absorption involves moving nutrients from the alimentary canal into the bloodstream. Finally, egestion ejects waste through the anus.

THE STOMACH

The stomach plays three roles in digestion. Firstly, its muscular walls contract to churn and crush food. Secondly, glands in the stomach wall release acidic gastric (stomach) juice. This contains an enzyme – pepsin – that digests proteins in food. The action of crushing and the pepsin turn swallowed food into a thick liquid called chyme. Thirdly, the stomach expands to store food for up to four hours. Its exit into the duodenum is guarded by a ring of muscle called the pyloric sphincter. This opens from time to time to release chyme into the duodenum.

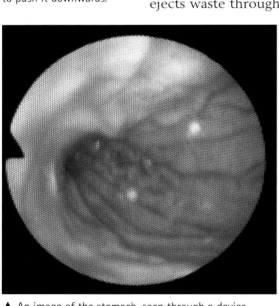

▲ An image of the stomach, seen through a device called an endoscope, clearly shows the slippery mucus that lines and protects the wall of the digestive system.

▶ The digestive system extends for about 9 metres from the mouth to the anus. Food enters through the mouth, where teeth and the tongue crush it into smaller pieces and the salivary glands lubricate it with saliva. Peristalsis takes the processed food from the oesophagus to the stomach, which partly digests and stores the food. The liver and pancreas release secretions into the small intestine, which completes digestion and absorption. The main function of the large intestine is to process waste.

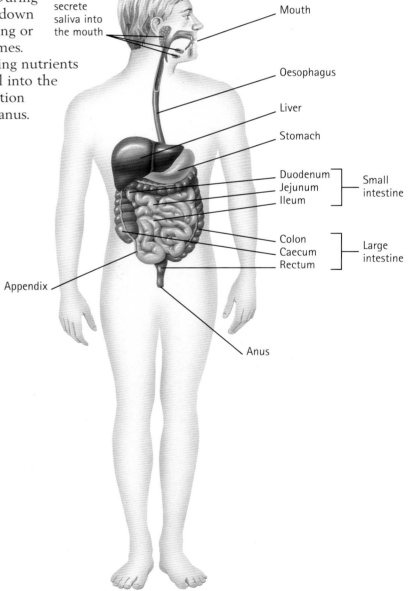

Salivary glands secrete saliva into the mouth

Mouth

Oesophagus

Liver

Stomach

Duodenum
Jejunum — Small intestine
Ileum

Colon
Caecum — Large intestine
Rectum

Appendix

Anus

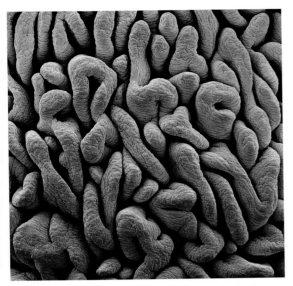

Villi line the ileum, which is part of the small intestine. This view magnified 18 times reveals a forest of these tiny flaps, each of which are about 1 mm long.

MAKING DIGESTION AN EFFICIENT PROCESS

The small intestine is coiled up in the abdominal cavity. It is between 6 and 7 metres long and holds food long enough for it to be digested and for simple nutrients to be absorbed into the bloodstream. The inner surface of the small intestine has many circular folds, which are covered by tiny projections called villi. Each villus contains a capillary network and a branch of the lymphatic system called a lacteal. Both carry nutrients away from the small intestine. Together, the circular folds and villi provide a massive surface area across which digested food can be absorbed quickly and efficiently.

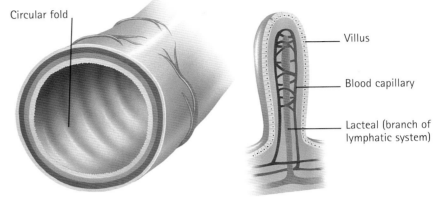

Circular fold

Villus

Blood capillary

Lacteal (branch of lymphatic system)

THE SMALL INTESTINE

The small intestine runs from the pyloric sphincter to the caecum of the large intestine. It is the most important part of the digestive system because most digestion and absorption takes place there. The small intestine is made up of three parts: the duodenum, the jejunum and the ileum.

The first part of the small intestine, the duodenum, is about 25 centimetres long. It receives chyme from the stomach. It also receives pancreatic juice from the pancreas whose enzymes digest carbohydrates, proteins and fats. Finally, it receives bile from the liver, which breaks up fats and makes them easier to digest. These secretions, along with intestinal juice secreted by the duodenal wall, make the food less acidic and allow enzymes to work more efficiently.

The jejunum is about 2.5 metres long. It produces enzymes that complete the digestion of carbohydrates, proteins and fats, in turn producing amino acids, fatty acids and simple sugars such as glucose.

The ileum is the last and longest part of the small intestine. The lining of the ileum is covered with finger-like villi. Sugars and amino acids pass through the villi into the bloodstream. There, they are carried to the liver for processing and then distributed to the body's cells. Fatty acids pass into lacteals – a part of the lymphatic system.

THE LARGE INTESTINE

The large intestine is 1.5 metres long and consists of the caecum, colon and rectum. Water is absorbed from the waste products of digestion as they pass through the colon. The waste forms semi-solid faeces, consisting of dead cells, fibre and bacteria. Faeces are stored in the rectum and then released through the anus.

▼ The lining of the colon is made up of two main types of cells. The cells shown in brown here (magnified 747 times) absorb water from faeces making them more solid. The rounded depressions shown in grey are cells that produce mucus.

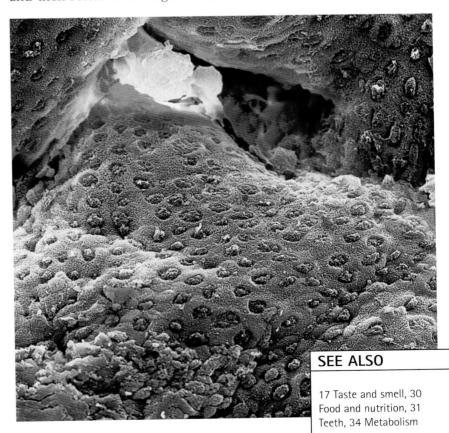

SEE ALSO

17 Taste and smell, 30 Food and nutrition, 31 Teeth, 34 Metabolism

METABOLISM

Metabolism is the combination of all the chemical reactions that take place inside the body's cells to maintain life. The liver plays a vital role in metabolism.

This boy is measuring his body temperature by using a heat-sensitive strip on his forehead. Metabolism releases enough heat to maintain the body at a constant temperature of about 37°C. An increase, or decrease, in body temperature means that the person is ill.

Day and night, thousands of different chemical processes take place inside each body cell. These metabolic reactions occur rapidly because they are catalysed (speeded up) by proteins called enzymes. These enzymes are controlled by DNA (genetic material) in the cell nucleus.

Metabolism has two parts that work together. Catabolism breaks down substances, such as glucose, to release energy. Anabolism uses raw materials to make complex substances that the body needs; for example, the production of proteins from their building blocks, amino acids. The energy released by catabolic reactions is used to power anabolic reactions. Metabolic rate is controlled by hormones (chemical messengers) such as those released by the thyroid gland.

FUNCTIONS OF THE LIVER

The dark red, wedge-shaped liver is the body's largest internal organ and occupies most of the upper right abdomen. Its billions of cells, called hepatocytes, perform more than 500 metabolic functions that control the blood's chemical makeup. The liver plays a major role in processing nutrients. This includes storing vitamins, especially A, D and B_{12}, and minerals, notably iron and copper – both needed to make haemoglobin (an oxygen-carrying substance in the blood). Hepatocytes produce bile, which helps digest fats in the small intestine. They also break down drugs, such as alcohol, and other poisonous chemicals. Its chemical content adjusted, blood leaves the liver through hepatic veins. Heat released by the liver helps the body maintain a constant temperature of 37°C.

THE LIVER

After digestion, nutrients are absorbed through the small intestine. This causes a rapid rise in levels of nutrients – particularly sugars, amino acids and lipids (fats) – in the blood. The liver controls blood nutrient levels to prevent this surge disrupting the activities of body cells. The liver has two blood supplies: one through the hepatic portal vein, rich in sugars and amino acids direct from the small intestine, and one through the hepatic artery, which delivers fats absorbed by the lymphatic system and then emptied into the blood. In the liver, excess sugars are stored as glycogen and excess amino acids are broken down to form urea. Excess fats are processed by liver cells or sent to adipose (fat) tissue for storage.

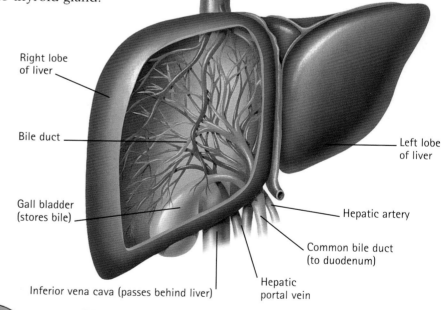

Inferior vena cava (to heart)

Right lobe of liver

Bile duct

Gall bladder (stores bile)

Left lobe of liver

Hepatic artery

Common bile duct (to duodenum)

Inferior vena cava (passes behind liver)

Hepatic portal vein

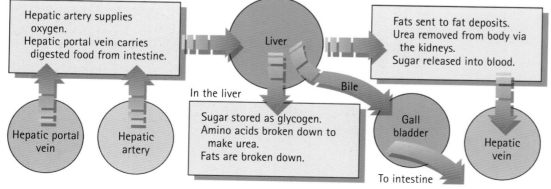

Hepatic artery supplies oxygen.
Hepatic portal vein carries digested food from intestine.

Liver

Fats sent to fat deposits.
Urea removed from body via the kidneys.
Sugar released into blood.

In the liver

Bile

Sugar stored as glycogen.
Amino acids broken down to make urea.
Fats are broken down.

Gall bladder

Hepatic vein

Hepatic portal vein

Hepatic artery

To intestine

SEE ALSO

26 Blood, 27 Lymphatic system, 30 Food and nutrition, 32–3 Digestion

WASTE DISPOSAL

The body constantly produces waste products as a result of chemical activity in its cells. Waste must be disposed of or it can build up and poison the body.

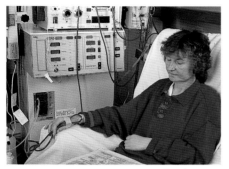

Kidney machines provide a lifeline for patients with kidney failure. As this patient's blood passes through the machine, a process called dialysis removes poisonous waste. To stay alive, she must be attached to the machine for four to eight hours, three times a week.

The process of waste disposal, called excretion, is carried out by excretory organs. Without them, waste would accumulate in tissue fluid, poisoning not only the cells but the whole body. Major excretory organs are the lungs, skin, liver and kidneys. The lungs excrete carbon dioxide, the waste product of energy release in cells, by breathing it out. The skin excretes water, salts and other wastes in sweat. The liver breaks down many poisonous substances, excretes wastes in the form of bile and produces urea, a waste made from excess amino acids. The kidneys excrete urea and other wastes in urine.

HOW THE KIDNEYS WORK

Kidneys process blood by excreting wastes such as urea and removing excess water. Together, wastes and water make urine. The 1.2 litres of blood received per minute through the renal (kidney) arteries is processed by nephrons, each consisting of a glomerulus, renal capsule and renal tubule. In a glomerulus, a liquid called a filtrate is filtered under pressure from the blood into the hollow renal capsule. Filtrate contains waste and excess water but also useful substances such as glucose and amino acids. As filtrate passes along the renal tubule, useful substances and most water are absorbed back into the blood. The remaining liquid, urine, is stored in the bladder, which empties several times a day.

Every day, about 180 litres of filtrate are filtered from the bloodstream, but only 1.5 litres of this is released as urine. The body's whole blood supply is processed by the kidneys about 60 times a day.

THE URINARY SYSTEM

The urinary system consists of two kidneys, two ureters, the bladder and the urethra. The two bean-shaped kidneys lie on the back wall of the abdomen, either side of the backbone and behind the stomach. Each consists of three layers: the cortex, medulla and inner renal pelvis. Cortex and medulla contain microscopic filtering units called nephrons that produce urine. This passes into the renal pelvis, trickles down the ureters and is stored in the bladder until it is released from the body through the urethra. In males the urethra opens at the tip of the penis; in females it opens between the legs.

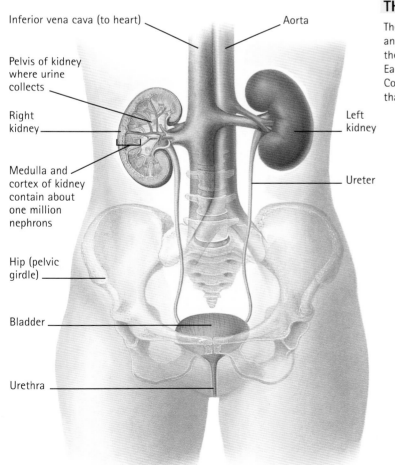

Inferior vena cava (to heart)

Aorta

Pelvis of kidney where urine collects

Right kidney

Left kidney

Medulla and cortex of kidney contain about one million nephrons

Ureter

Hip (pelvic girdle)

Bladder

Urethra

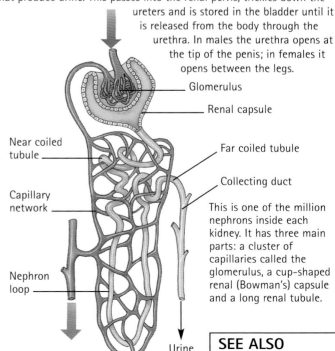

Glomerulus

Renal capsule

Near coiled tubule

Far coiled tubule

Collecting duct

Capillary network

This is one of the million nephrons inside each kidney. It has three main parts: a cluster of capillaries called the glomerulus, a cup-shaped renal (Bowman's) capsule and a long renal tubule.

Nephron loop

Urine

SEE ALSO

26 Blood, 27 Lymphatic system, 32–3 Digestion

REPRODUCTION

Reproduction ensures that the human species does not become extinct. The male and female reproductive systems enable men and women to have children.

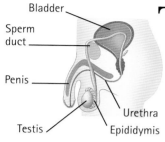

Bladder
Sperm duct
Penis
Testis
Urethra
Epididymis

Testes make millions of sperm a day. During sexual intercourse, the penis gets erect and is put into the female's vagina. Sperm travel along the sperm duct and out of the penis.

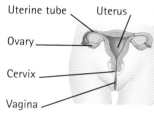

Uterine tube
Uterus
Ovary
Cervix
Vagina

The ovaries contain a store of eggs, one of which is released each month. If it is fertilized by a sperm cell, it develops into a baby in the uterus. At birth, the baby passes out through the vagina.

The reproductive system does not become active until puberty during the early teens. Male and female reproductive systems differ, although both produce sex cells. Sex cells are made by a type of cell division called meiosis. Sex cells contain only 23 chromosomes (genetic material) in their nucleus, half the number found in other cells. The male sex cells, called sperm, are made in the two testes. More than 250 million sperm are made each day. The female sex cells, called eggs or ova, are produced in the two ovaries before birth. After puberty, one egg is released each month – ovulation – and the body prepares for possible pregnancy. Sperm and egg are brought together by an intimate act called sexual intercourse. The man inserts his penis into his partner's vagina and releases millions of sperm that swim towards the fallopian tubes. If sexual intercourse happens within 24 hours of ovulation, a sperm may penetrate the egg. This is called fertilization. The sperm's nucleus (23 chromosomes) fuses with that of the egg (23 chromosomes); the combined genetic material (46 chromosomes) gives the blueprint for a new human being.

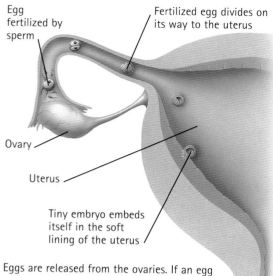

Egg fertilized by sperm
Fertilized egg divides on its way to the uterus
Ovary
Uterus
Tiny embryo embeds itself in the soft lining of the uterus

Eggs are released from the ovaries. If an egg meets a sperm, it is fertilized. As it travels along the fallopian tube, the fertilized egg divides repeatedly. In seven days, the egg arrives in the uterus. It is now a hollow ball of cells.

CONCEPTION

Conception is the time between fertilization and implantation. As the fertilized egg passes along the fallopian tube it divides repeatedly to form a ball of cells called a conceptus. After seven days, the conceptus sinks into the soft lining of the uterus and becomes an embryo. If the two daughter cells separate when the fertilized egg first divides, the two cells will develop independently and result in identical twins. If two eggs are released during ovulation and both are fertilized by sperm, they will produce non-identical, or fraternal, twins.

HOW A BABY DEVELOPS IN THE WOMB

After fertilization, the fertilized egg travels to the uterus. What started as a single cell becomes a foetus made up of billions of cells. Development occurs within a fluid-filled sac, protected within the uterus. Food and oxygen pass through the umbilical cord from the placenta, where blood from the foetus and mother come into close contact.

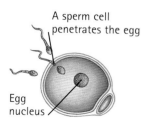

A sperm cell penetrates the egg
Egg nucleus

1 During fertilization, the nucleus of a sperm cell fuses with the nucleus of the egg to produce a fertilized egg.

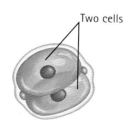

Two cells

2 Approximately 36 hours after the egg is fertilized, the egg has divided once, resulting in two cells.

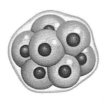

3 About 72 hours after fertilization there are 16 cells. In a few days, the ball of cells will settle in the uterus.

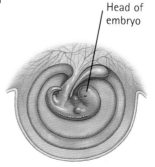

Head of embryo

4 After four weeks, the embryo is floating in a fluid-filled sac. The heart is beating and the brain has started to develop.

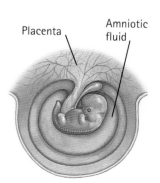

Placenta
Amniotic fluid

5 After five weeks, the embryo is the size of an apple pip. It has buds that will become arms and legs. The tail is shrinking.

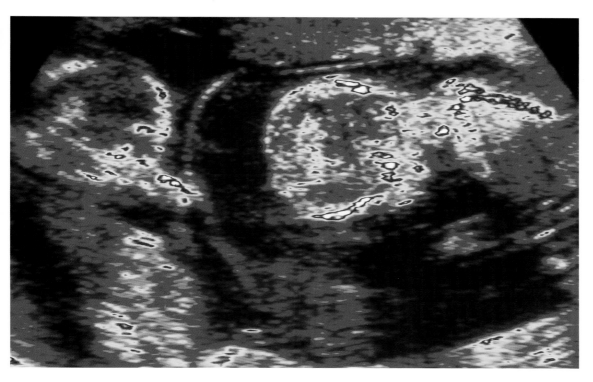

The picture above shows a healthy baby boy. The human body never grows as fast as it did in the womb. If growth continued at the same rate, a baby would be two kilometres tall by its first birthday.

PREGNANCY

Pregnancy is the time between conception and birth. For the first two months the developing baby is called an embryo. After this, when the organs are working, it is called a foetus. Amniotic fluid surrounds and protects the foetus. The growing baby is kept alive by the placenta, which is attached to the uterus. Inside the placenta, food and oxygen pass from the mother's blood to that of the foetus, and wastes pass in the opposite direction. The umbilical cord carries blood between placenta and foetus.

BIRTH

About 38 weeks after fertilization, the uterus starts to contract. This process, called labour, usually begins about 12 hours before the birth. Powerful contractions push the baby out through the vagina, and the baby takes its first breath of air.

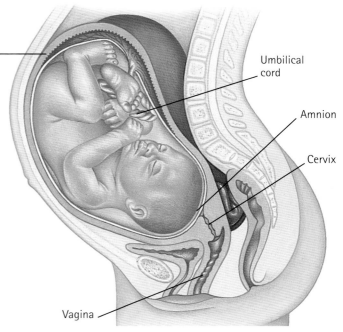

Uterus

Placenta

Uterus

Umbilical cord

Amnion

Cervix

Vagina

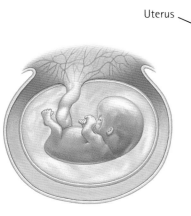

6 After eight weeks, the embryo – now called a foetus – is about the same size as a strawberry and has developed tiny fingers and toes.

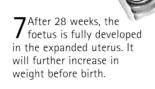

7 After 28 weeks, the foetus is fully developed in the expanded uterus. It will further increase in weight before birth.

8 At full term, about 38 weeks after fertilization, the foetus has moved its head downward in preparation for birth.

SEE ALSO

2–3 Body organization, 38 Growth and development, 39 Genes and chromosomes

GROWTH AND DEVELOPMENT

Growth and development – from birth to adulthood – follow a fixed pattern in the first 20 years of life. By the age of 40, the first signs of ageing begin to appear.

Growth and development occur simultaneously. Growth is an increase in size. Development is where cells specialize to perform specific functions. During its first year, an infant is totally dependent on his or her parents for food and protection. However, the infant is already starting to develop skills such as talking, walking and interacting with others. These skills become more obvious and develop further as an infant gets older.

▲ Mother and baby make eye contact. This bonding process starts from the very moment a baby is born. Being held makes babies feel secure; they respond by smiling and making noises. Bonding reinforces the natural feelings parents have for their children.

▼ Every person follows the same pattern of growth and development, with slight differences between the development of the male and female reproductive systems. After rapid growth in the first year of life, children grow steadily until their early teens. Then, during puberty, the body grows rapidly and takes on an adult appearance. By the age of 20, the body has completed its growth.

PUBERTY AND ADOLESCENCE

Puberty is a time of rapid growth that leads to sexual maturity. It starts around the age of 11 in girls and about 13 in boys. In both sexes, armpit and pubic hair grows. A girl's body becomes more rounded. Breasts develop and the hips become wider. Her ovaries start to release eggs and menstruation begins. A boy's body becomes more muscular and hairy. His shoulders widen, his voice deepens and the testes start to produce sperm. Puberty is part of adolescence, which also involves mental changes. These changes make a young adult become more independent and have sexual feelings.

Face and skull aged 6

Face and skull aged 16

Two photos of the same person taken at different ages show how the face changes shape between the ages of 6 and 16. The bones of the face – as shown by the shape of the skulls – grow rapidly during late childhood.

AGEING

The body ages fairly rapidly after the age of 40. As cells become less efficient, the skin becomes more wrinkled, muscles less powerful, bones more brittle, senses less acute and the hair thins and turns grey. Eventually, one or more body systems stop working and the person dies.

Age 30–34

Age 2

Age 6

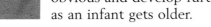

Age 10–12

Age 20–22

SEE ALSO

15 Communication, 22–3 Hormones, 36–7 Reproduction, 39 Genes and chromosomes

GENES AND CHROMOSOMES

Chromosomes are found in the nucleus of nearly every cell. Each chromosome contains sets of instructions called genes.

DNA

Deoxyribonucleic acid, or DNA, stores the information needed to build a cell. Together, cells make up a human body. DNA molecules are coiled up and packaged into thread-like chromosomes. There are 46 chromosomes in the nucleus of most human cells. DNA molecules are organized into two linked strands that spiral around one another, forming a structure called a double helix. The strands are held together by four different chemicals called bases. The precise sequence of bases along a DNA molecule provides coded instructions for cell construction and operation.

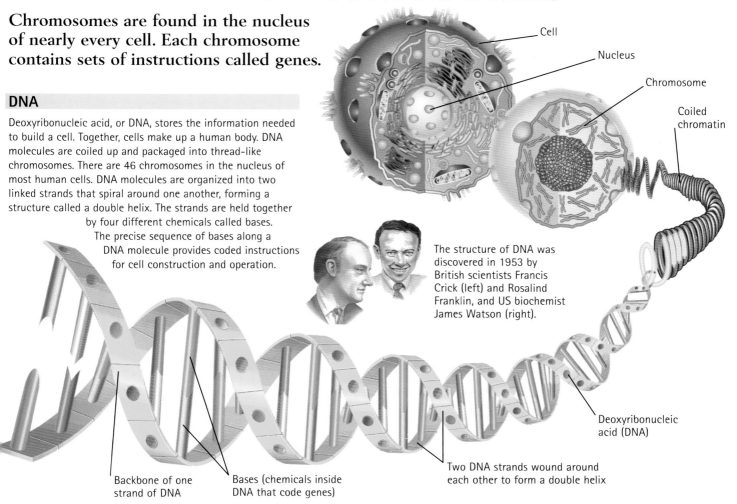

Cell

Nucleus

Chromosome

Coiled chromatin

The structure of DNA was discovered in 1953 by British scientists Francis Crick (left) and Rosalind Franklin, and US biochemist James Watson (right).

Deoxyribonucleic acid (DNA)

Backbone of one strand of DNA

Bases (chemicals inside DNA that code genes)

Two DNA strands wound around each other to form a double helix

D NA molecules are made up of sections called genes. There are about 100,000 different genes in a human body, and together they control the way our bodies grow and function. Each gene instructs a cell to make a specific protein. In turn, proteins build every cell in our bodies and produce the substances or release the energy they need to work. Identical twins have the same sets of genes, but everyone else has a set that is unique. A person's genes are an individual combination of the genes of his or her parents. Genes occur in pairs – for instance, there is a gene which controls eye colour. A child inherits one eye-colour gene from his or her mother, and another eye-colour gene from his or her father. This determines what colour eyes he or she has. The Human Genome Project, currently being carried out by scientists worldwide, aims to identify every human gene to find out what it controls.

CHROMOSOMES

Chromosomes contain thousands of genes. Genes are passed on from parents to their offspring. In the ovaries and testes, a process of cell division called meiosis makes sex cells (eggs and sperm) that contain 23 chromosomes. At fertilization, a sperm cell joins the egg to produce the full complement of 46 chromosomes. One pair of chromosomes, the sex chromosomes, differ from the other 22 pairs of chromosomes. While they carry genes, they are not the same in both sexes. Males have a longer (X) chromosome paired with a shorter (Y) chromosome. Females have two X chromosomes. The presence of XY chromosomes in the embryo ensures that male reproductive organs are formed.

▼ An electron micrograph reveals eight of the 46 chromosomes found inside the nucleus of a human cell. This image was taken during mitosis. In this type of cell division, the chromosomes become much shorter and thicker.

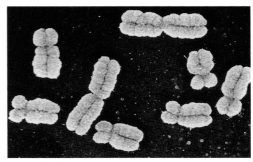

SEE ALSO

36 Reproduction, 38 Growth and development, 40 Bacteria and viruses

BACTERIA AND VIRUSES

Bacteria are micro-organisms, whereas viruses are packages of chemicals. Some bacteria and viruses, called pathogens, can infect the body and cause disease.

Diseases such as the common cold are spread from person to person through tiny droplets in the air. If an infected person sneezes, droplets filled with micro-organisms are projected out of their nose into the air at high speed. If other people breathe them in they may become infected.

▼ A virus reproduces by attaching itself to a cell (1). It injects its genetic material into the cell (2), which interferes with the cell's metabolism (3) and forces it to make new viruses (4). The new viruses then break out of the dying host cell (5).

Bacteria are single-celled micro-organisms that are much simpler than the cells that make up animals and plants. Bacteria are everywhere. They thrive in the soil, the air and even in our digestive systems. Most bacteria are harmless organisms, but some species, called pathogens, are harmful and cause disease. Pathogenic bacteria are divided into three groups according to their shape. Cocci are spherical and cause sore throats, boils and pneumonia. Bacilli are shaped like rods and cause typhoid and salmonella. Spirochetes are spiral and cause Lyme disease and syphilis.

Bacteria invade the body in various ways: in droplets that are breathed in from the air, through cuts in the skin, in water or food that is swallowed and through the reproductive system during intercourse. Once inside the body, bacteria feed and divide and release toxins that harm human cells. Usually, the immune system detects bacteria and destroys them. Infections can also be treated by a course of antibiotics. They can be prevented by immunization, proper hygiene, clean drinking water, and by cleaning wounds with antiseptic.

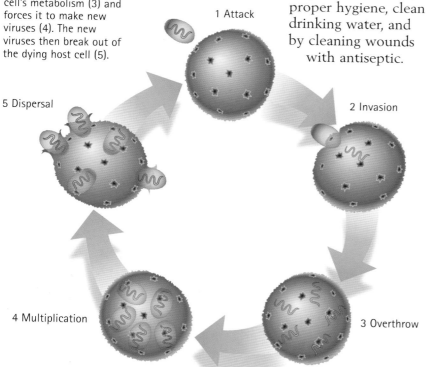

1 Attack

2 Invasion

3 Overthrow

4 Multiplication

5 Dispersal

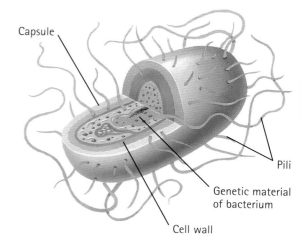

Capsule

Pili

Genetic material of bacterium

Cell wall

Bacteria are prokaryotes (simple cells). Unlike eukaryotes (complex cells), prokaryotes do not contain a nucleus or other organelles. They are surrounded by a cell wall and a protective outer capsule. The rod-shaped bacterium, or bacillus, above is covered with fine threads called pili. Pili are used to attach the bacterium to food or other cells.

VIRUSES

Viruses cause many human diseases, including cold sores (herpes), the common cold, measles and mumps. Viruses are non-living packages of chemicals, consisting of a strand of genetic material – either DNA or RNA – surrounded by a protein coat. In order to reproduce, viruses invade a host cell and copy themselves. They cause disease by either destroying their host cell or through the response of the immune system to them, which may result in fatigue, fever or even severe tissue damage. Most viruses are dealt with by the immune system without ill effects. Some infections, such as herpes, can 'hide' inside the body, re-emerging periodically to cause further outbreaks. Some viral infections can be prevented by immunization, but most are difficult to treat using drugs. Antibiotics are totally ineffective. One viral disease, human immunodeficiency virus (HIV), attacks the immune system itself. In time, opportunistic infections attack the defenceless body, causing acquired immunodeficiency syndrome or AIDS. There is no cure for HIV at present.

SEE ALSO

41 The immune system,
42 Disease

THE IMMUNE SYSTEM

The human body is under constant threat from pathogens. The immune system provides a formidable defence against these disease-causing micro-organisms.

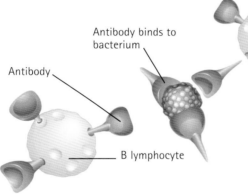

Red blood cell

White blood cell

Bacterium

Blood vessel

There are three ways the body defends itself from invading pathogens. Physical barriers include the skin, and tears and saliva, which contain the bacteria-killing chemical lysozyme. Pathogens that do get through are engulfed by white blood cells called phagocytes, destroyed by natural killer cells in the lymphatic system or targeted by antimicrobial proteins. Lastly, pathogens are tackled by the most powerful line of defence – the immune system.

1 The immune system is made up of defensive white blood cells found in the lymphatic system and in blood. The white blood cells shown above are called B lymphocytes. They recognize antigens (markers) on the surface of bacteria that have invaded the bloodstream.

English doctor Edward Jenner (1749-1823) did the first vaccination. He used fluid taken from a blister caused by a mild infection called cowpox to vaccinate a boy against a related but fatal disease called smallpox. When exposed to smallpox the boy survived.

► A white blood cell called a macrophage (here magnified 2,340 times) engulfes a pathogenic protist (blue). This protist causes a tropical disease called leishmaniasis, resulting in painful ulcers. It is spread to humans by biting sandflies that are infected with the protist.

Antibody binds to bacterium

Antibody

B lymphocyte

2 The B lymphocytes multiply rapidly, producing plasma cells. These cells release antibodies, which attack the invading bacteria. Antibodies lock on to the antigens and disable the bacteria.

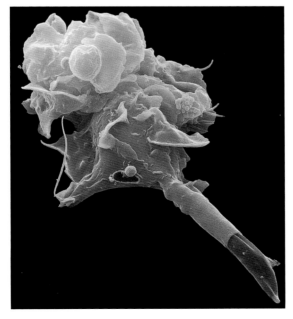

THE IMMUNE RESPONSE

The immune system consists of cells called lymphocytes, which recognize chemicals called antigens on the pathogens' surfaces. B cells or B lymphocytes release antibodies that lock onto specific antigens, disable pathogens and mark them for destruction. T cells or T lymphocytes identify and directly destroy pathogens. Memory cells 'memorize' antigens. The immune system takes a few days to respond to a new antigen – the primary response. The person may become ill. The next time, memory cells remember antigens and cause a rapid response by B and T lymphocytes – the secondary response – destroying invaders. The person is immune to the disease.

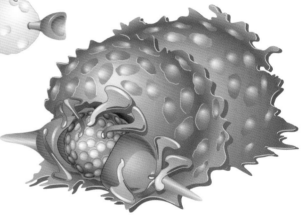

3 The disabled bacteria are now marked for destruction. White blood cells, called macrophages, seek them out and destroy them. Some lymphocytes, called memory cells, can memorize the invader's identity.

IMMUNIZATION (VACCINATION)

Immunization primes the immune system to act rapidly against particularly nasty pathogens. A person is injected with a vaccine containing altered pathogens. These stimulate the immune system to produce antibodies without causing illness. If the real pathogen later invades the body, the immune system responds immediately. Active immunization has significantly decreased infectious diseases worldwide. In 1975, for example, it eradicated smallpox.

SEE ALSO

26 Blood, 27 Lymphatic system, 40 Bacteria and viruses, 42 Disease

DISEASE

Disease occurs when there is a breakdown in the body's normal functioning. It may be caused by external agents, such as bacteria, or internal disruption, such as cancer.

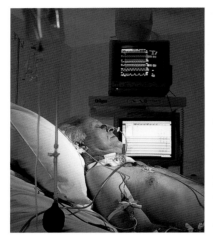

A patient in a hospital intensive care unit has his heart rate and blood pressure monitored and is given oxygen. The screen (top) shows his heart rate (green), blood pressure (red and light blue), blood oxygen levels (dark blue) and breathing rate (white).

Many diseases are short-lived and cure themselves; others are more serious and require drugs or surgery to tackle them. Diseases fall into two groups: infectious and non-infectious. Infectious diseases are caused by organisms called pathogens, particularly bacteria and viruses. Some are caused by single-celled protists, such as malaria and sleeping sickness; by fungi, such as athlete's foot; or by parasitic worms, such as tapeworms that live and feed in the small intestine.

Pathogens invade the body through various routes including the mouth or nose and through cuts. If they are not immediately challenged by the immune system, pathogens multiply, attack tissues and cause infection. Those infections, such as colds or measles, that are passed on very easily, are called contagious. They may result in epidemics where many people in the same location are affected. Some infectious diseases, such as sleeping sickness, are passed on by other animals who become known as vectors.

The scolex, or 'head' of the 10-metre-long beef tapeworm is magnified 22 times. Its suckers grip the wall of the small intestine. Humans become infected by eating raw beef.

NON-INFECTIOUS DISEASES

Non-infectious diseases are the most common cause of death in developing countries. People cannot catch these diseases; they are caused by instructions contained within genes, by hazardous chemicals in the environment, by lifestyle factors such as smoking, poor diet or lack of exercise or by an interaction of these factors. The commonest non-infectious diseases are heart disease and cancers. Some non-infectious diseases are inherited. These include sickle-cell anaemia, where red blood cells do not work properly, and cystic fibrosis, where breathing and digestion are affected.

African tsetse flies feed on human blood by pushing their tubular, sucking mouthparts into the skin. These flies also carry a protist parasite that causes trypanosomiasis, or sleeping sickness. As the fly feeds, parasites enter a person's bloodstream and invade the lymphatic system and brain. An infected person suffers confusion and extreme tiredness and eventually dies. Infection is diagnosed through blood samples (far right) and can be treated with drugs.

Parasite that causes sleeping sickness in bloodstream

Human skin

Tsetse fly uses proboscis to bite through skin and into blood vessel

Red blood cell

EXERCISE AND FITNESS

A fit body is one that is more likely to be, and remain, healthy. Fitness is achieved through regular exercise, reducing stress and eating a balanced diet.

Fitness is a person's ability to carry out a wide range of everyday activities without any undue stress, tiredness or gasping for breath. Unfortunately, modern lifestyles tend to make humans less fit. Whereas everyday activities such as hunting would have kept our ancestors fit, modern humans use buses or cars rather than walk and spend hours sitting in front of the television or computer. This lack of activity makes people more prone to lifestyle problems such as heart disease. Fortunately, regular exercise can improve both fitness and health. Among other benefits, it reduces body fat and weight, makes the heart and lungs more efficient, improves posture and muscle tone, reduces the risk of heart disease, reduces stress and allows a person to sleep more soundly.

TYPES OF FITNESS

Exercise improves fitness in three areas: stamina, muscle fitness and flexibility. Stamina, or cardiovascular endurance, is the ability of the heart and blood vessels to deliver oxygen efficiently to the body's cells. It is improved by regular aerobic exercise, such as running or cycling.

Muscle fitness has two parts. Muscle strength – the force a muscle produces – is improved by, for example, weight training. Muscle endurance, the muscle's ability to contract repeatedly in a short time, is improved, for example, by running or cross-country skiing.

Flexibility is the ability of muscles to stretch and the joints to move freely and without discomfort through a full range of movement. Activities such as yoga and swimming improve flexibility.

A varied exercise programme will improve all aspects of fitness. Before exercise, it is important to warm up to help prevent damage to muscles and other tissues. Cooling down after exercise, preferably by stretching, is also important.

▲ Stretching forms an important part of an exercise routine, especially during cooling down. This woman is supporting the man as he stretches muscles in his arms, the side of his body and his legs. Stretching makes muscles and joints more flexible, increasing the body's range of movement as well as preventing muscle stiffness.

▶ During aerobic exercise, muscles need more glucose and oxygen to provide extra energy. The heart speeds up to pump more blood to the muscles. Breathing rate increases to get more oxygen into the blood. Blood is diverted from other body parts, such as the digestive system, to hard-working muscles. Regular exercise improves fitness by increasing the efficiency of heart, lungs and muscles.

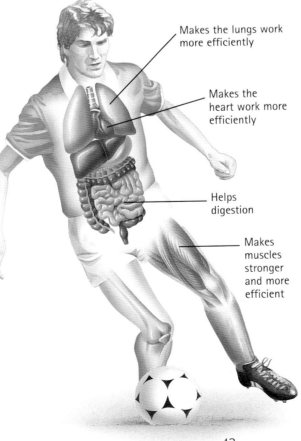

Makes the lungs work more efficiently

Makes the heart work more efficiently

Helps digestion

Makes muscles stronger and more efficient

▲ Aquarobics provides the benefits of aerobic exercise but reduces strain on the knees because the body is supported in water.

SEE ALSO

24–5 Heart and circulation, 28–9 Lungs and breathing

MEDICINE

Medicine is the study, treatment and prevention of human diseases. Modern medicine enables people to live longer and healthier lives.

Liquid medicines such as syrups make swallowing drugs easy.

Capsules and tablets are common ways to give drugs to a patient.

Drugs can be injected into the blood or under the skin using needles.

Inhalers and eye drops send drugs rapidly to their target area.

Sometimes drugs need to be released into the bloodstream slowly. Slow-release capsules contain hundreds of tiny, hollow balls called pellets, which contain the drug. Pellets are colour-coded according to how thick their outer coat is. Thin-coated pellets release their contents into the stomach soon after swallowing; thick-coated pellets release the drug later in the small intestine.

Medicine deals with all aspects of diseases, including their causes, prevention and treatment. It was only in the 20th century that the effective cure and control of disease became possible. For the first time there were skilled, well-trained doctors and nurses. A wide range of drugs, such as bacteria-killing antibiotics, became available, as did immunization to eliminate childhood diseases, such as polio. Doctors had new ways of diagnosing their patients' illnesses. Patients could survive surgery because it was carried out in clean, germ-free conditions, using sterile instruments and with the patient anaesthetized. Many new surgical methods, such as transplants, were developed.

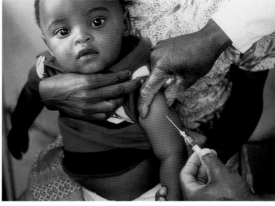

This child is being injected with the DPT vaccine. It will immunize, or protect, him against three diseases: diphtheria, pertussis (whooping cough) and tetanus.

PREVENTATIVE MEDICINE

Preventative medicine deals with the prevention of diseases. Clean drinking water and efficient sewage-treatment systems are public-health measures that prevent the spread of diseases through water. Health education informs people about the health risks of smoking cigarettes or drinking too much alcohol and about the benefits of regular exercise and a balanced diet. Immunization protects children against serious diseases. Screening programmes detect diseases such as cancer or high blood pressure before they cause symptoms.

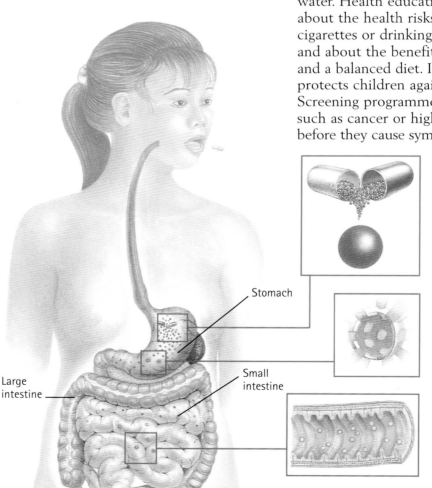

Large intestine

Stomach

Small intestine

1 Within an hour of swallowing, digestive enzymes in the stomach dissolve the outer capsule so that it releases its colour-coded pellets.

2 Pellets with the thinnest outer coat dissolve in the stomach. The drug they contain is absorbed through the stomach wall into the bloodstream.

3 A few hours after swallowing, enzymes break open pellets with a thicker coat. Their content is absorbed through the wall of the small intestine.

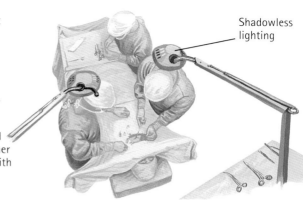

◄ Doctors use different pieces of equipment to look for signs of disease to make a diagnosis. Here a doctor is using an ophthalmoscope to examine a woman's eye. The instrument may reveal problems with vision, or the eye's blood vessels may show whether she has any problems with circulation.

Shadowless lighting

DIAGNOSIS AND TREATMENT

A doctor makes a diagnosis to determine what is wrong with a patient. To do this, the doctor follows a series of logical steps. First, the doctor listens to the patient talk about the symptoms; that is, those things the patient feels are wrong. The doctor asks the patient to give an account of the illness, saying how long the patient has had the symptoms and whether the patient has experienced them before. Second, the doctor examines the patient to look for identifiable signs of disease. This may involve pressing an affected part of the body or using instruments such as a stethoscope to listen to the heart and lungs, a sphygmomanometer to measure blood pressure, or an ophthalmoscope to look into the eye. The doctor may be able to make a diagnosis straight away but may need more information. This may come, for example, from tests to analyse blood or urine or from body images such as X-rays or CT scans.

If the doctor can make a diagnosis, the patient can often be treated. If the doctor is still unsure or feels that the disease is too serious to deal with, he or she may refer the patient to a specialist. Treatment often uses drugs, which are chemicals that alter the working of the body to get rid of the cause of the disease. Other forms of treatment are bed rest, physiotherapy to aid recovery from muscle or bone injury, radiotherapy to destroy tumours (growths) or a surgical procedure.

ALTERNATIVE THERAPIES

Many alternative therapies are becoming accepted by conventional medicine. Some, such as acupuncture and herbalism, have ancient origins. Others, such as osteopathy and homeopathy, are more recent.

Alternative therapies tend to treat the whole person rather than individual symptoms. Acupuncture uses fine needles to restore health. Herbalism uses traditional plant extracts to treat a person. Yoga involves meditation and posture correction to relieve stress and improve flexibility. Osteopathy uses manipulation and massage. Homeopathy treats a disease with drugs that produce the same symptoms as the disease.

In a typical operation, doctors use instruments to open a patient's body in order to diagnose or treat a disease. The patient lies on an operating table in an operating theatre. The doctors wear masks and gowns to avoid passing on any infections during the operation. This patient has been given a general anaesthetic in order to be completely unconscious and not feel anything.

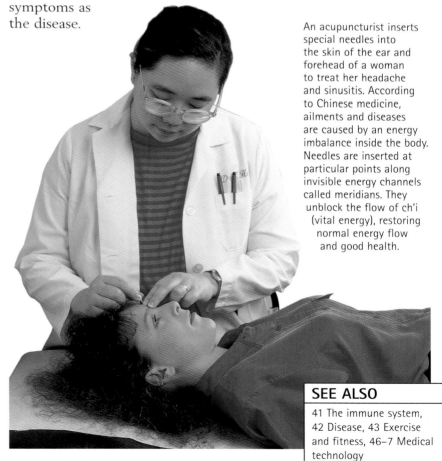

An acupuncturist inserts special needles into the skin of the ear and forehead of a woman to treat her headache and sinusitis. According to Chinese medicine, ailments and diseases are caused by an energy imbalance inside the body. Needles are inserted at particular points along invisible energy channels called meridians. They unblock the flow of ch'i (vital energy), restoring normal energy flow and good health.

SEE ALSO

41 The immune system, 42 Disease, 43 Exercise and fitness, 46–7 Medical technology

MEDICAL TECHNOLOGY

Modern medicine owes much to advances in technology in the 20th century. New techniques enable doctors to diagnose and treat diseases more effectively.

Wilhelm Roentgen (1845–1923) discovered X-rays. X-rays reveal the hard parts of the body, such as bone. For the first time doctors were able to look inside a living body without cutting it open.

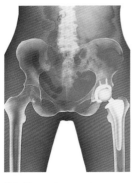

This X-ray image shows an artificial hip joint. In the past, a diseased hip joint used to stop a person from walking. Today, it can be removed and replaced by a prosthesis (artificial part) made of stainless steel and plastic.

▶ Lasers produce a concentrated beam of light radiation. They have many uses, including cutting through tissue, and destroying tumours (growths). Here a doctor aims a laser into the eye of a patient using a retinal camera. The laser beam is delivered in a series of short bursts. In eye surgery it can be used to mend a detached retina or to seal blood vessels to stop them bleeding.

Medical technology allows doctors to treat diseases and to perform complicated surgery under safer conditions. Imaging techniques produce a clear, electronic picture of the inside of the body so that doctors can pinpoint problems. Endoscopy enables doctors to look directly through a viewing tube inside the body to see what is wrong.

Together, imaging and endoscopy mean doctors can perform minimally invasive, or 'keyhole', surgery, entering the body through the smallest of incisions (cuts). This minimizes tissue damage and makes recovery time for the patient shorter. The use of lasers, such as the laser scalpel, to cut through tissue, remove growths and seal blood vessels is much more effective than standard surgical methods.

Computers are now a major part of medicine. They are used in scanning to generate and store images and to transmit them elsewhere. Virtual-reality systems are used to train doctors in surgical techniques without having to touch a patient.

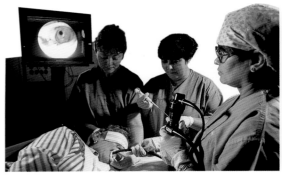

Doctors look inside the body using an endoscope to make a diagnosis or carry out treatment. Here, doctors insert an endoscope through the mouth to examine a patient's stomach. The view inside appears on the screen.

ENDOSCOPY

Doctors use endoscopes to look inside the body to diagnose or treat diseases. Modern endoscopes are narrow and flexible and are inserted either through body openings into the digestive, respiratory, urinary or reproductive systems, or through incisions in the skin into body cavities. Endoscopes use long, thin optical fibres to illuminate and transfer the images to a video monitor, which the doctor looks at while he or she conducts the examination. The endoscope may also have, for example, tiny forceps to carry out a biopsy (the taking of a tissue sample) for diagnosis.

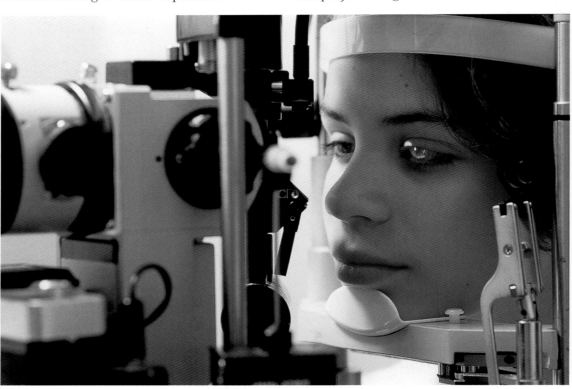

LOOKING INSIDE THE BODY

A computerized tomography (CT) scanner combines X-rays and a computer to produce clear 'slices' through the body that reveal far more about the body's tissues than do X-rays alone. Here a patient's head is going to be scanned. He lies down on the scanner table and remains still while scanning takes place. As the scanner rotates around the patient, bursts of X-ray beams, each lasting a fraction of a second, pass through his head at different angles. The way in which X-rays are absorbed by different parts of the head is recorded by detectors.

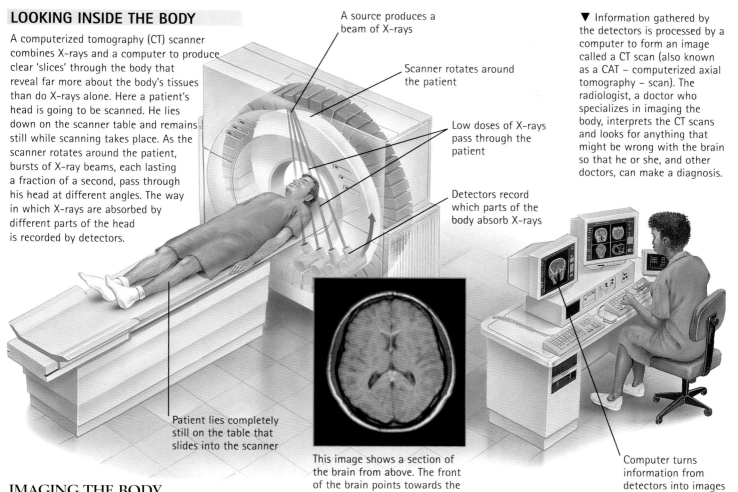

A source produces a beam of X-rays

Scanner rotates around the patient

Low doses of X-rays pass through the patient

Detectors record which parts of the body absorb X-rays

▼ Information gathered by the detectors is processed by a computer to form an image called a CT scan (also known as a CAT – computerized axial tomography – scan). The radiologist, a doctor who specializes in imaging the body, interprets the CT scans and looks for anything that might be wrong with the brain so that he or she, and other doctors, can make a diagnosis.

Patient lies completely still on the table that slides into the scanner

This image shows a section of the brain from above. The front of the brain points towards the top of the page.

Computer turns information from detectors into images

IMAGING THE BODY

Imaging techniques enable doctors to look inside the body to make diagnoses and plan treatment without having to cut open the body. The pioneer of imaging was Wilhelm Roentgen, who discovered X-rays in 1895. This was the only useful imaging method until the 1970s. Since then a new generation of techniques has been developed. Although they work in different ways, all scan a particular body region piece by piece and use a computer to make two- or three-dimensional images.

Ultrasound is the most common of the imaging techniques. It uses inaudible, high-frequency sound waves that are reflected from body parts. It is a safe method for observing unborn babies and viewing moving parts, such as blood flow through the heart.

CT scanning uses X-rays. PET – positron-emission tomography – scans use radioactive substances that, when they are injected into the body, give off radiation and reveal the parts of the human body where cells are active.

REPLACEMENT PARTS

Today, many diseased or damaged body parts can be replaced. The earliest replacement parts were prostheses such as wooden legs. Modern prostheses, such as plastic arms with moving fingers, are more lifelike. Internal replacement parts are a relatively recent development.

Transplantation takes a living organ from a donor and inserts it into the patient. Kidney transplants, for example, are made to treat people with kidney failure. The body's immune system regards transplanted organs as 'foreign' and attempts to reject them. The transplant patient has to take drugs that prevent rejection by reducing the effectiveness of the immune system.

Implants are artificial internal devices that are not rejected by the immune system. They include artificial joints that can replace diseased joints and electronic pacemakers that regulate heart rate.

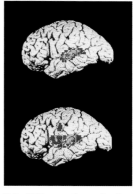

This PET scan shows brain areas at work. The top scan shows a person listening to words: the brain's hearing area (yellow) is working. Below, the person is listening to words and repeating them. Both hearing area and speech area (green) are activated.

SEE ALSO

44–5 Medicine

INDEX